the Pink Drink Book

A Cocktail Recipe Book for Women

by Jaclyn Wilson Foley
Editor of Bartender Magazine

Printed in the United States of America

First Printing August 2003

10 9 8 7 6 5 4 3 2 1

Copyright 2003 by Jaclyn Wilson Foley

Published by Foley Books

www.pinkdrinkbook.com

ISBN 0-9702863-1-7

To my son Ryan Peter Foley and

my husband Raymond Peter Foley,

who have both contributed to this book and

most importantly to my happiness.

And to the 150,000 plus readers and

followers of Bartender Magazine

who sent us recipes, ideas and inspiration

that helped to contribute to the success of

the Pink Drink Book.

Welcome!

Thank you for purchasing "The Pink Drink Book"

Bartending is an art. It's the art of making cocktails and mixing with people. It's the art of hospitality and creativity. It's the art of listening and understanding. It's the art of sales and service. It's fashion. It's society and sensibility. It's patience and pouring.

When tending bar, you learn a tremendous amount about people, both good and could do without! In my case, 99% good and only 1% could do without. "The Pink Drink Book" is my look at bartending and cocktails from a woman's viewpoint. I do believe in creativity for all—get crazy, get creative and pull out all the stops. Let's decorate, use fun glassware, great garnishes and have fabulous times!

It's called BARTENDING and we are bartenders, not barmaids, goddesses, bargirls, Ms. Mixologists, or Master Mixologists. We are good, hard-working and creative Bartenders.

In the selection of brands for "The Pink Drink Book," I have chosen top-of-the-line products. Always use the best ingredients to insure the best tasting cocktails. Using the best makes the best! There are no substitutions.

The bar business has been my life for the last 22 years. I now have the opportunity to share with you some tips, clues, cocktails and, at the same time, help my friends at "a time for ME." (See page 11.)

Please always remember never drink to excess. Moderation is the key in all things. Use good judgement not only for yourself but when serving guests. Drinking and driving do not mix at all, ever! The cocktails in "The Pink Drink Book" are for your pleasure in moderation.

I have included many websites and other books to assist you or advance your knowledge in this great art — BARTENDING. Enjoy "The Pink Drink Book."

Acknowledgments

I'd like to thank my sponsors for their contribution to "The Pink Drink Book"

Jim Beam Brands Worldwide, Inc. with special thanks to Mike Donohoe, Kathleen DiBenedetto, Heather Mitchell, and Chris Gretchko for VOX Vodka, Knob Creek Bourbon, and DeKuyper Cordials.

Vox Vodka Vox Vodka is a pristine, ultra-premium spirit imported from the Netherlands and created for a chilled cocktail glass. Vox is a spirit of exceptional smoothness, unsurpassed clarity and a cool finish. Vox is distilled from 100 per cent wheat, chosen for its mildness and ability to give the vodka a remarkable smoothness. The clarity of Vox is attained by using demineralized water produced through a careful process of reverse osmosis to remove all traces of color and odor. Vox is then distilled five times, at a very high proof, to remove any elements that could taint the final product.

Knob Creek Daring to set new standards, Knob Creek Bourbon has established itself as an exceptional whiskey. Handcrafted in limited quantities using time-honored recipes, aged a full nine years, and hand-bottled at an honest 100 proof, Knob Creek Bourbon has established itself as an exceptional whiskey. Daring to set new standards, Knob Creek even dares to look entirely different, housed in a unique flask-shaped bottle.

DeKuyper Cordials For more than 300 years, DeKuyper has been the brand to turn to for fresh and original liqueurs. DeKuyper has survived this ever-changing market by combining its rich traditional expertise with modern innovations and a healthy dash of imagination. From the punch of Original Peachtree Schnapps, the fiery bite of Hot Damn! to the mouthwatering tang of Pucker Sour Apple Pucker Schnapps, John DeKuyper & Son has created a magical array of exciting flavors and colors.

JSH&A Public Relations with special thanks to Laura Dihel, Kate McCutcheon, and Jim Kokoris.

Future Brands LLC with special thanks to Alan Mervish.

Bacardi USA, Inc. with special thanks to Lydia Holland, Celio Romanach, Joy Suchlicki, Mark Dean, Ria Campbell, Sumindi Peiris, Michael Curry, Christine Moll, Monica Garaitonandia, John Gomez, Joe Metevier, and Gonzalo de la Pezuela for Bacardi Rums, Bombay Sapphire Gin, Disaronno

Amaretto, Dewars Scotch, Martini & Rossi Vermouths, and Drambuie.

Bacardi Rum How is it that Bacardi rum is the most popular spirit in the world today? Unique taste. Outstanding quality. Unequaled mixability. And a natural complement to so many great foods. It's a rum as rich in taste as in its own history. Because the rum bares a proud family name, to this day the quality of Bacardi rum has never been allowed to falter. Bacardi Rum is one of America's favorite drinks and is also one of the most mixable. It can be used with all mixes and juices and is a great product to use when creating your own special drink.

Bombay Gin/ Bombay Sapphire Gin The recipe for Bombay Gin dates back to 1761, and the botanicals - including coriander, lemon peel, angelica, licorice, anise, juniper, almonds and cassia bark - are imported from around the world. The spirit used in Bombay's production comes from a distillery in Ayrshire, Scotland and the soft, pure water is drawn from the Welsh Hills. Bombay owes its growing success to a uniquely slow and unhurried distillation process that ensures the consistently high standard of Bombay Gin.

Unlike other gins which boil their botanicals with the spirit, the Bombay Sapphire spirit is distilled alone. To achieve the unique flavor of Bombay Sapphire, the spirit passes through the botanicals in vapor form. This allows each delicate aroma to be fully absorbed. The result is Bombay Sapphire Gin, a complex yet subtle taste sensation.

Disaronno Amaretto Disaronno is made using only the highest quality ingredients like absolute alcohol, burnt sugar and the pure essence of seventeen selected herbs and fruits soaked in apricot kernel oil. This special recipe hasn't changed since 1525.

Dewar's White Label Dewar's White Label is a sophisticated blended scotch whisky that's honeyed and spicy, yet light and smoky. Taste the smoothness that could only come from 40 of Scotland's finest single malts and grain whiskies and over 150 years of bold, Dewar's Scottish tradition.

Martini & Rossi Vermouths In 1863 three partners joined together to found a company which today is the market leader in the Vermouth industry. They took over an established 18th century firm that had been producing Vermouth in Torino, Italy, and by the end of the same year, were exporting the first Martini Vermouth for sale in the United States. Martini & Rossi Vermouth is a true aperitif - that is a wine incorporating aromatic substances and bitter plants, it is differentiated from other aromatized wines by the presence of bitter plants which stimulate digestive juices. Martini & Rossi's success is based upon its reputation as the finest Vermouth in the world - one well earned and carefully preserved.

Drambuie From the Gaelic meaning "the drink that satisfies", Drambuie is a rich combination of fine aged scotch whiskies, heather honey and the secret ingredients of the original recipe.

Rèmy Amerique with special thanks to Jane Scott and Susan Mitchell for Cointreau.

Cointreau Cointreau has been a worldwide legend since its creation in 1849. The innovation of the Cointreau family over 150 years has made Cointreau one of the world's most famous and successful liqueurs. It is the authentic choice of many top bartenders, and you will always find Cointreau in the smartest and most fashionable bars. The warm amber coloured bottle with its rounded shoulders and red ribbon has remained virtually the same for 150 years, yet has retained its impact and appeal.

Diageo with special thanks to Debbie Greene for Jose Cuervo Tequila.

Jose Cuervo For over 200 years, the Jose Cuervo family has produced the finest tequila in the world. This untamed spirit, steeped in legend and mystique, can trace its origins back as far as the 1770's. An entire lifetime dedicated to the pursuit of tradition and heritage allows Jose Cuervo to reign supreme and dominate the world. Jose Cuervo Especial has established the "gold standard" by becoming the number one tequila in the world.

Schieffelin & Somerset with special thanks to Christy Frank for Hennessy Cognac.

Hennessy Cognac In 1765, Richard Hennessy laid the foundation of a priceless collection made up of his most exceptional eaux de vie. For more than seven generations, the same family of Cellar Masters has watched over Hennessy's stocks. Today, it is Yann Fillious who continues the family tradition, often using eaux de vie set aside by his grandfather in the cognacs he creates for Hennessy. This commitment to tradition and continuity is the essence of what sets Hennessy V.S., V.S.O.P. Privilege, X.O., Private Reserve, Paradis Extra and Richard Hennessy cognacs apart from the crowd.

Charles Jacquin, et Cie., Inc. with special thanks to Robert Cooper and Kevin O'Brien for Chambord.

Chambord Chambord is made in small batches to ensure that only the ripest fruits are used. Chambord cultivates the finest framboises noires (small black raspberries) which are the essence of the liqueur. Chambord is a world-class liqueur enjoyed by the world's most discriminating tastes, and the same family has owned and produced Chambord for generations. Each successive son has passed down a passion for quality that has remained unchanged from the very beginning.

C&C International with special thanks to Alan B. Lewis for Carolans Irish Cream, Irish Mist Liqueur, and Tullamore Dew Irish Whiskey.

Carolans Carolans is produced in Clonmel in County Tipperary. The place name is derived from the Irish words "Clauin Meala", which means "Vale of Honey". This is very appropriate for Carolans, which includes honey in the recipe. All Irish Cream liqueurs combine cream, Irish whiskey, spirits and flavours for their taste, but there the similarities end. The technological process used in making Carolans is unique, ensuring a rich creamy taste and superior shelf life. Also, the flavours are different in Carolans, in particular, the use of honey.

Irish Mist Imagine the wonderful taste of aged Irish whiskey, blended with honey, herbs and other spirits to a perfect smoothness. Now visualize that golden liqueur in a sleek new bottle with gracefully swirling motif and jewel-like label, perfectly representing the contemporary Ireland of the 21st century. That's Irish Mist - a smart, versatile drink for today's generation yet with years of quality and history behind it. Enjoy it on its own, with ice, mixed into a memorable cocktail, or as the vital ingredient in an Ultimate Irish Coffee.

Tullmore Dew One of Ireland's finest and most widely distributed whiskeys, Tullamore Dew was first distilled in 1829 in the small town of Tullamore in County Offaly in the heart of Ireland. The name derives from the initials of an early owner, Daniel E Williams - DEW. Tullamore Dew is a favourite among Irish whiskeys for its distinctive, accessible taste, enjoyed on its own, over ice or with a little water. Connoisseurs describe Tullamore Dew as "subtle, smooth and with a pleasant maltiness combined with charred wood undertones and the natural flavour of golden barley".

The Cherry Marketing Institute with special thanks to Cheryl Kroupa for the fabulous maraschino cherry.

You have all made me "pink" with pride to publish this book and to benefit a worthy cause. I can't thank you all enough.

a time for ME

Caring for Women with Cancer

a time for ME *Caring for Women with Cancer* is a group of professional women from the healthcare and business community who have come together to provide a comprehensive program to benefit women who are dealing with the trauma of cancer. **a time for ME** offers women with cancer a complimentary one day retreat or weekend where they can regroup their energies and focus on a positive tomorrow. These programs are complimentary to women whom have been diagnosed with cancer and live in Monmouth or Ocean counties in New Jersey. We will gladly include women from other regions who have been financially sponsored.

a time for ME is just what it sounds like, a weekend away at a lovely spa. Your stay will be a unique personal experience. From the moment you arrive you'll find yourself immersed in mountain beauty or Seashore Victorian charm. Here in this quiet setting you will become relaxed, physically rejuvenated and spiritually renewed. This weekend is totally complimentary!

A mandatory orientation meeting is held prior to our departure to the Spa. A group of 8-10 women and 2 facilitators will start their weekend on Friday morning. Transportation will be provided to out-of-state spas. All participants will be given their choice of salon services. **a time for ME** recipients may participate in most of the Spa activities when available.

Most reservations are double occupancy. Dress is very casual. Bring work-out clothes, swim suit and hiking boots.

Sunday morning we all convene after breakfast for a group discussion. We arrive home Sunday afternoon, after a comprehensive weekend of pleasure.

Day Spa

The day is held at a local spa, which has been carefully selected to meet the needs of our women. Generally we have an intimate group of women who will be joined by a member of the **a time for ME** committee.

This relaxing respite will encompass approximately a 5 hour day. A sampling of what may be included on your day spa experience are facials, pedicures, massages, manicures, yoga, nutrition seminar and make-up application. For those in need, a new hairstyle may also be offered. A light spa meal will be served. Dress is casual.

a time for ME *Caring for Women with Cancer* is an independent organization. Since there are no administrative costs, donations are used directly in support of the women.

a time for ME *Caring for Women with Cancer* is a federally recognized, non-profit, tax exempt, and publicly supported organization. As such, our only funding is through private donations and the committee's fund-raising efforts. Such donations are vital to the continuance of this program.

Donations are accepted in memory and in honor of. We will gladly send an acknowledgment of your donation upon request.

PLEASE SEND YOUR
DONATIONS TO:

a time for ME
PO Box 364, Brielle, NJ 08730

Anyone can make a referral to **a time for ME**. Most referrals come from: Physicians, Healthcare Professionals, Support Groups, Hospitals Personal Referrals. All referrals are kept confidential. When making a referral, we ask that your candidate be aware that you are making the referral.

Please call or fax all referrals to:
a time for ME
Phone: 732-701-0506 or Fax: 732-701-0989

www.atimeforME.org

What This Weekend Meant to ME

*Written by one of the women who spent
a weekend away due to generous supporters.*

Smiling...with others who share my pain
Hugging...to let each one know we're okay
Caring...the personnel who touched us with healing hands
Compassion...for the sadness we carry in our lives
Relief...from our private hell
Beauty...we are all beautiful again
Happiness...to have the privilege of meeting each and
every woman I shared this special weekend with
Memories...to carry with us.

Table of Contents

See back of book for fabulous bar gifts and for writing your own recipes.

Facts on Liquor & Proof

THE MEANING OF PROOF

Proof spirit, underproof, and overproof are terms difficult to explain in easy language since they are arbitrary standards set up by governments for collection of revenue.

Proof spirit is defined by law to be spirit which at 51°F. weighs $^{12}/_{13}$ of an equal measure of distilled water. At 51°F. it has a specific gravity of .92308. It is a mixture of about 57% pure alcohol and 43% water.

An underproof mixture of alcohol and water contains less than 100% of the mixture called proof spirit. So in 100 gallons of 20 underproof whiskey there is 80 gallons at proof strength and 20 extra gallons of water.

Overproof whiskey contains more alcohol and less water than proof spirit.

This proof chart shows these differences.

Britian & Canada		American		Alcohol by % Vol.
	75.25	200	Proof	100.0%
	Overproof			
50	Overproof	172	Proof	86.0%
30	Overproof	149	74.5%	
	Proof	114.2	Proof	57.1%
12.5	Underproof	100	Proof	50.0%
30	Underproof	80	Proof	40.0%
50	Underproof	57	Proof	28.5%
100	Underproof	0	Proof	0.0%

Charts & Measures

MEASUREMENTS

	Metric	Standard
1 Dash	0.9 ml	$\frac{1}{32}$ ounce
1 Teaspoon	3.7 ml	$\frac{1}{8}$ ounce
1 Tablespoon	11.1 ml	$\frac{3}{8}$ ounce
1 Pony	29.5 ml	1 ounce
1 Jigger	44.5 ml	1-$\frac{1}{2}$ ounces
1 Wineglass	119.0 ml	4 ounces
1 Split	177.0 ml	6 ounces
1 Miniature (nip)	59.2 ml	2 ounces
1 Half Pint	257.0 ml	8 ounces
1 Tenth	378.88 ml	12.8 ounces
1 Pint	472.0 ml	16.0 ounces
1 Fifth	755.2 ml	25.6 ounces
1 Quart	944.0 ml	32.0 ounces
1 Imperial Quart	1.137 Liter	38.4 ounces
1 Half Gallon	1.894 Liter	64.0 ounces
1 Gallon	3.789 Liter	128.0 ounces

Dry Wine and Champagne

	Metric	Standard
Split ($\frac{1}{4}$ bottle)	177.0 ml	6 ounces
Pint ($\frac{1}{2}$ bottle)	375.2 ml	12 ounces
Quart (l bottle)	739.0 ml	25 ounces
Magnum (2 bottles)	1.534 Liter	52 ounces
Jeroboam (4 bottles)	3.078 Liter	104 ounces
Tappit-hen	3.788 Liter	128 ounces
Rehoboam (6 bottles)	4.434 Liter	
Methuselah (8 bottles)	5.912 Liter	
Salmanazar (12 bottles)	8.868 Liter	
Balthazar (16 bottles)	11.829 Liter	
Nebuchadnezzar (20 bottles)	14.780 Liter	
Demijohn (4.9 gallons)	18.66 Liter	

DEPARTMENT OF THE TREASURY
BUREAU OF ALCOHOL, TOBACCO AND FIREARMS
DISTILLED SPIRITS

Bottle Size	Equivalent Fluid oz.	Bottles/ Per Case	Liters/ Per Case	U.S. Gallons Per Case	Corresponds To
1.75 Liters	59.2	6	10.50	2.773806	½ Gallon
1.00 Liters	33.8	12	12.00	3.170064	1 Quart
750 ml.	25.4	12	9.00	2.377548	⅘ Quart
500 ml.	16.9	24	12.00	3.170064	1 Pint
200 ml.	6.8	48	9.60	2.536051	½ Pint
50 ml.	1.7	120	6.00	1.585032	1, 1.6, 2 oz.

DEPARTMENT OF THE TREASURY
BUREAU OF ALCOHOL, TOBACCO AND FIREARMS
WINE

Bottle Size	Equivalent Fluid oz.	Bottles/ Per Case	Liters/ Per Case	U.S. Gallons/ Per Case	Corresponds To
4 Liters	135				1 Gallon
3 Liters	101	4	12.00	3.17004	⅘ Gallon
1.5 Liters	50.7	6	9.00	2.37753	⅖ Gallon
1 Liter	33.8	12	12.00	3.17004	1 Quart
750 ml.	25.4	12	9.00	2.37763	⅘ Quart
375 ml.	12.7	24	9.00	2.37753	⅘ Pint
187 ml.	6.3	48	8.976	2.37119	⅖ Pint
100 ml.	3.4	60	6.00	1.58502	2, 3, 4 oz.

Calories & Carbohydrates

	Calories	Carbo-hydrates
Ale	72	
Beer (12 oz. bottle or can)	144	11.7
Light Beer	110	6.9
Bourbon		
80 proof, distilled	65	trace
86 proof, distilled	70	trace
90 proof, distilled	74	trace
94 proof, distilled	77	trace
100 proof, distilled	83	trace
Brandy		
80 proof, distilled	65	trace
86 proof, distilled	70	trace
90 proof, distilled	74	trace
94 proof, distilled	77	trace
100 proof, distilled	83	trace
Champagne		
Brut (4 fl. oz.)	92	2.1
Extra Dry	97	2.1
Pink	98	3.7
Coffee Liqueur		
53 proof	117	16.3
63 proof	107	11.2
Creme de Menthe, 72 proof	125	14.0
Gin		
80 proof (1 oz.)	65	0.0
86 proof (1 oz.)	70	0.0
90 proof (1 oz.)	74	0.0
94 proof (1 oz.)	77	0.0
100 proof (1 oz.)	83	0.0
Rum		
80 proof (1 oz.)	65	0.0
86 proof (1 oz.)	70	0.0
90 proof (1 oz.)	74	0.0
94 proof (1 oz.)	77	0.0
100 proof (1 oz.)	83	0.0

	Calories	Carbo-hydrates
Scotch		
80 proof, distilled	65	trace
86 proof, distilled	70	trace
90 proof, distilled	74	trace
94 proof, distilled	77	trace
100 proof, distilled	83	trace
Tequila		
80 proof, distilled	64	0.0
86 proof, distilled	69	0.0
90 proof, distilled	73	0.0
94 proof, distilled	76	0.0
100 proof, distilled	82	0.0
Vodka		
80 proof (1 oz.)	65	0.0
86 proof (1 oz.)	70	0.0
90 proof (1 oz.)	74	0.0
94 proof (1 oz.)	77	0.0
100 proof (1 oz.)	83	0.0
Whiskey		
80 proof (1 oz.)	65	0.0
86 proof (1 oz.)	70	0.0
90 proof (1 oz.)	74	0.0
94 proof (1 oz.)	77	0.0
100 proof (1 oz.)	83	0.0
Wine		
Aperitif (1 oz.)	41	2.3
Port (1 oz.)	41	2.3
Sherry (1 oz.)	41	2.3
White or red table (1 oz.)	29	1.2
Non-Alcoholic		
Club soda (1 oz.)	0	0.0
Cola (1 oz.)	12	3.1
Cream soda (1 oz.)	13	3.4
Fruit-flavored soda (1 oz.)	13	3.7
Ginger ale (1 oz.)	9	2.4
Root beer (1 oz.)	13	3.2
Tonic water (1 oz.)	9	2.4

Tools To Tickle Your Drinks

You need the proper tools to make outstanding drinks. Below are a few of the tools that will help to make you a real pro.

Bar Spoon A long spoon for stirring cocktails or pitchers.

Blender Blending drinks or crushing ice. Remember to save your blade by always pouring in the liquid before the ice.

Cocktail Shaker and Mixing/Measuring Glass There are countless designs to choose from, but the standard is the Boston. It's a mixing glass that fits snuggly into a stainless steel cone.

Ice Bag To crush ice use a rubber mallet and a lint free or canvas ice bag, often referred to as a Lewis Ice Bag.

Ice Bucket Should have a vacuum seal and the ability to hold three trays of ice.

Ice Scoop/Tongs/Ice Pick Never use your hands to pick up ice, use a scoop or tongs. The ice pick can help you unstick ice or break it up.

Jigger/Measuring Glass Glass or metal, all drinks should be made using these bar tools. Remember that drinks on the rocks and mixed drinks should contain no more than 2 oz. of alcohol.

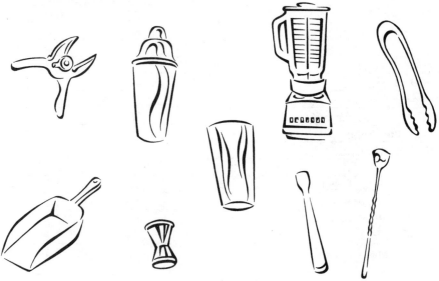

Knife and Cutting Board A sturdy board and a small, very sharp paring knife are essential to cutting fruit garnishes.

Muddler Use this small wooden bat or pestle to crush fruit, herbs or cracked ice. Muddlers come in all different sizes and are used for making Stixx drinks.

Napkins/Coasters To place a drink on, hold a drink with and for basic convenience.

Pitcher of Water Keep it clean. Someone always wants water and you certainly will use it.

Pourer A helpful way to pour directly into the glass. A lidded spout helps keep everything but the drink out.

Stirrers/Straws Use them to sip, stir and mix drinks. Glass is preferred for the mixer/stirrer.

Strainer The strainer, quite simply, prevents ice from pouring out of the shaker. The two most common types in use are the Hawthorne, with its distinctive coil rim it is most often used when pouring from the metal part of the Boston Shaker, and the Julip, a perforated metal spoon like strainer used when pouring from the glass part of the Boston.

Wine/Bottle Opener They come in all shapes and sizes, the best is the industry standard Waiter's opener. It can open cans as well as snap off those bottle tops and has a sharp blade.

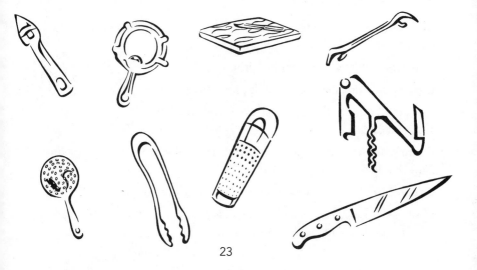

Dressing Up The Drink – Garnishes

You drink with your eyes, and the prettier you can make a drink, the more appealing it is. You can have a great tasting drink but if it does not look good then no one will want to taste it. In this case, you do judge a book by its cover and a drink by its garnish. Below are some ideas for garnishes and a simple lesson on cutting shapes of some basic fruits and vegetables. But remember: use your imagination and personality; you can get wild with garnishes. Always make sure your garnishes are fresh and clean.

Types of Cut

Slice A thinly cut portion, with a bit of peel on top, or half a wheel

Twist Made by using a paring knife to cut away a thin portion of peel, which will naturally twist

Wedge A triangular cut portion of the fruit or veggie

Wheel A whole slice, the fruit or veggie from peel to peel

Types of Garnish

Apples, Apricots, Peaches and Plums They look best sliced. Peaches in particular make a great champagne garnish

Bananas Slices or wheels. Make sure the bananas are not too ripe

Celery Whole stalk with flower

Chocolate sticks They make a great stirrer and garnish in one. (And I know these are available at Bloomingdales)

Cinnamon sticks Great for hot drinks

Cloves Add them whole to hot drinks

Cocktail Onions Whole onions are usually used in a Gibson Cocktail

Coffee Beans Three beans are usually dropped into Sambuca, sometimes flamed. I do not recommend flaming

Cucumber A Slice or a twist makes a very nice decoration

Flowers Rose pedals, small baby orchids or any other flower look great in most tall cocktails and adds a great visual effect

Fresh Herbs Mint is the most popular, but you can use Cilantro, Basil, Rosemary, and Thyme. Many herbs work well in Bloody Mary's and of course Mint is commonly known as being in the Mint Julip or Mojito. But remember, Mint can be used in a garnish as you see fit. It looks nice and it smells great. Use your imagination!

Lemons Twist, slices, wheels and wedges

Limes Twist, slices, wheels and wedges

Maraschino Cherries The fun fruit, it looks good, tastes good and adds value to any drink or desert. The Maraschino originates from an Italian liqueur which used the local "Marasca" cherry as its base. Originally brought to the United States in the 1890's from regions of Yugoslavia and Italy and by 1920 the American maraschino had replaced the foreign versions. American producers used a domestic sweet cherry called the Royal Anne cherry and eliminated the use of liquor in the processing, substituting it with almond oil. The modern day Maraschino is primarily grown in Oregon, Washington and Michigan and is characterized by its bright, uniform color and fruit cherry flavor with just a mere hint of almond.

Olives Whole black and green, both can be stuffed with almonds, anchovies, blue cheese, pimentos

Oranges Twist, slices, wheels and wedges

Pineapples Wedges, also use the whole pineapple as a serving container

Pink Grapefruit Though bitter, large grapefruit slices or wheels can add a burst of flavor

Raspberries Whole or muddled

Salt Table salt, sea salt, kosher salt, are used to coat the rim of the glass and are mostly for Margarita's or a Salty Dog. You can also add half sugar to the salt, which makes for an interesting taste. Colored salts are also available and fun

Sugar Can be used to coat drinks. Cubes can be used in Champagne drinks, and there are colored sugars available as well

Strawberries Sliced and hung on the side of the glass

"Toys" Non-edible plastic mermaids, Barrel of Monkeys, baby ducks, umbrellas, fancy straws and stirrers and little boats add a fun element to a drink. Make sure they are small enough to fit in the drink and large enough so you can't swallow them. Remember these "toys" are not for children under 21

Cutting Fruit

Different kinds of fruit are used to garnish different kinds of drinks.
REMEMBER to wash all fruit and vegetables before cutting.

Lemon Twist 1) Cut off both ends. 2) Using a sharp knife or spoon, insert between rind and meat carefully separating. 3) Cut skin into ¼" strips.

Pineapple 1) Cut off top and bottom. 2) Cut pineapple in half. 3) Cut in half again. 4) Cut ½" slices. 5) Cut wedges.

Celery 1) Cut off bottom of celery, also, you may cut off top. 2) If leaf is fresh, you may use this as garnish. 3) Cut celery stalk in half.

Oranges 1) Cut oranges in half. 2) Slice orange into half moon cuts. 3) Half moon cut.

Limes 1) Cut ends of lime. 2) Slice lime into half. 3) Cut in half moons.

Wedges (Lemon/Limes) 1) Slice lime in half. 2) Cut halves flat down and half again. 3) Cut to ¼" to ½" wedges.

Mixers & Enhancers

Here's a great way to add creativity and sparkle to a drink, by adding a great mix or enhancer. Changing the color, texture and taste of the alcohol with a juice or other product can make it memorable. Mixers and enhancers should also be on hand for people who do not drink alcohol. (Be sure to check our section on non-alcoholic drinks). When using juices, make sure you check the expiration date and use the liquid quickly after opening, there is nothing worse than a juice that has gone bad. Don't let your enhancer be a distracter.

Fruit Juice

Apple Juice Bottled apple juice is the best. Check dates.

Clamato Juice A mixture of clam and tomato juice.

Cranberry Juice Cocktail Excellent bottled.

Grapefruit Juice Fresh is best, but like orange juice some carton and frozen varieties can do the job.

Lime Juice If you can not get fresh squeezed I highly recommend Rose's Lime Juice.

Orange Juice fresh squeezed is the best but there are great frozen and carton varieties available.

Pineapple Juice Bottled is best.

Tomato Juice Bottled juice is best. For Bloody Mary's try using V-8.

Other Mixers

Try your local grocery store for a variety of new and mixed juice drinks like cran-apple. Ocean Spray has a ton of new juice mixes, go out and try some, have fun and experiment. You may surprise yourself.

SODA:
Cola or diet cola, Dr. Pepper, Ginger Ale, Lemon-Lime Soda, Root beer, Seltzer Water or Club Soda, Tonic Water

* Check your local store; there are many regional specific sodas that can add zest to a drink.

OTHER MIXERS:
Beef Bullion, Cappuccino, Clam Juice, Coco Lopez Cream of Coconut, Coffee, Espresso, Half and Half, Heavy Cream, Honey, Ice Cream, Lemon juice or lemon mix and Tea.

ENHANCERS:
Angostura Bitters

Chocolate Syrup A good quality fine chocolate syrup can make a great chocolate martini and add flavor to any ice cream drink

Egg Whites Not recommended for use due to food safety reasons

Falernum Syrup A rum based syrup from Barbados with a refined infusion of lime laced with fine cane syrup and 'botanicals' including almonds and cloves

Fruit Syrups There are many available such as strawberry, raspberry and other berries. For more information on the syrups available contact Monin (www.monin.com)

Horseradish

Orgeat Syrup Flavored with almonds and orange flavored water

Peychauds Bitters Available from the Sazerac Company (504-831-9450)

Rose's Grenadine

Rose's Lime Juice

Worcestershire Sauce

Pousse-Café

Pousse-Cafè is French for "after coffee". They are layered specialty drinks. By adding the ingredients in order of their specific gravity they will remain separate and the result is a colorful rainbow effect. I have included two sample recipes as well as a specific gravity chart and a color layering guide. Use these to create your very own Pousse-Cafes!

Angel's Kiss
1 oz. DeKuyper Dark Crème de Cacao
Top with cream

Traffic Light
⅓ DeKuyper Green Crème de Menthe
⅓ Carolans Irish Cream
⅓ Cointreau

Specific Density Chart

Product	Proof	Density
DeKuyper Coffee Liqueur	53	1.1389
DeKuyper Almond Liqueur	56	1.1294
DeKuyper Butterscotch Schnapps	30	1.1225
DeKuyper Crème de Cassis	40	1.1211
DeKuyper Dark Crème de Cacao	54	1.1141
DeKuyper Apple Pucker	30	1.0944
DeKuyper Cheri-Beri Pucker	30	1.0937
DeKuyper Coconut Amaretto	48	1.0925
DeKuyper Anisette Liqueur	60	1.0921
DeKuyper Green Crème de Menthe	60	1.0885
DeKuyper Grape Pucker	30	1.0864
DeKuyper Crantasia Schnapps	30	1.0863
DeKuyper Blueberry Schnapps	30	1.0863
Disaronno Amaretto	56	1.085
DeKuyper Apple Schnapps	48	1.0844
DeKuyper Banana	56	1.0822
Benedictine	80	1.0725
DeKuyper Blue Curacao	54	1.0704
DeKuyper Hazelnut Liqueur	56	1.0685
Galliano	60	1.065
DeKuyper Cinnamon Schnapps	60	1.0632
DeKuyper Blackberry Brandy	70	1.0552
DeKuyper Coffee Brandy	70	1.0543
DeKuyper Apricot Brandy	70	1.0437
DeKuyper Cactus Juice Schnapps	30	1.0430
DeKuyper Cherry Brandy	70	1.0392
Cointreau	80	1.0385
B & B	80	1.0245
DeKuyper Ginger Brandy	70	1.0060
Southern Comfort	80	.09933

Layering Guide By Color

Product	Color
Grenadine	Red
DeKuyper Creme de Cassis	Red
DeKuyper Creme de Cacao, Brown	Brown
DeKuyper Coffee Liqueur	Brown
DeKuyper Peach Schnapps	Clear
DeKuyper Creme de Banana	Yellow
DeKuyper Anisette	Clear
DeKuyper Crème de Menthe, Green	Green
DeKuyper Crème de Menthe, White	Clear
DeKuyper Melon	Green
DeKuyper Cherry Brandy	Red
DeKuyper Apricot Brandy	Gold
Galliano	Yellow
Disaronno Amaretto	Tawny
Benedictine	Gold
DeKuyper Peppermint Schnapps	Clear
DeKuyper Spearmint Schnapps	Clear
Irish Mist	Gold
Cointreau	Clear
DeKuyper Sloe Gin	Red
B & B	Gold
Chambord	Purple
Drambuie	Gold
Southern Comfort	Gold

Glassware

Today, about 40 per cent of all cocktails are served in a martini glass. Can you serve a martini in a wine glass? Sure, serving cocktails in different types of glasses will not change the taste of the drink, just the serving glass. But a beer glass should always be used to serve beer and a cream drink glass should be washed at least twice. Champagne always in a champagne glass or flute. But also remember that glassware can add flare to a drink, so be creative. The following is a list of some common glassware that can bring vitality to your concoctions:

Brandy Snifters Smaller sizes of the glasses, which come in sizes ranging from $5\frac{1}{2}$ to 22 oz, are prefect for serving cognac, liqueurs and premium whiskeys. The larger sizes provide enough space for a noseful of aroma and the small stems on large bowls allow a cupped hand to warm the liquid

Champagne Glass A narrow version of the standard wine glass has a tapered bowl to prevent those tiny bubbles from escaping and is usually never more than half filled. Also preferable for any sparkling liquid, including ciders

Cocktail or Martini Glass Perfect for martinis and manhattans, remember that the stem is not just for show: it keeps hands from warming the drink. Available in 3 to 6 oz sizes

Collins Glass The fraternal twin brother of the highball is often frosted and a tad taller, which adds a tropical look to many fruity drinks

Champagne Glass   **Collins Glass**

Brandy Snifters   **Cocktail or Martini Glass**

Highball Glass **Red Wine Glass**

Coolers **Hurricane Glass**

Coolers These large capacity tumblers are taller and hold a lot of ice for larger concoctions. They have become popular as of late for non-alcoholic and extra volume highballs

Highball Glass Extremely versatile glass available in many sizes and used for almost any drink. Usually clear and tall, the most popular sizes range from 8 to 12 ounces

Hurricane Glass Tropical fruit drinks and bloody Marys are perfectly suited for these 16 to 23 oz tall, curved glasses

Red Wine Glass The wine glass with the slightly larger bowl which allows the red vintages to breathe but keeps the aroma trapped

Rocks Glasses These "old fashioned" glasses hold from 6 to 10 ounces and are used for on-the-rocks presentations. Double rocks will run between 12 and 15 ounces

Sherry Glass Small 2 to 3½ once stemmed glasses are perfect for sherry, port and aperitifs

Shot Glass The old stand by can also be used as a measuring glass and is a must for every bar

White Wine Glass Smaller wine glasses are preferable, though sizes range from 5 to 10 ounces

White Wine Glass

Sherry Glass

Rocks Glass **Shot Glass**

Types of Drinks

There are seven basic ways of preparing a drink; you can blend, build, shake, stir, mix, layer, or muddle. Within these ways of preparing though, come many types of drinks, and here are a few interesting ones. First off, I will quickly go over some of the older types of drinks.

They are:

Aperitif A light alcohol drink served before lunch or dinner, sometimes bitter

Cobbler A tall drink usually filled with crushed ice and garnished with fruit or mint

Crusta Served in a wine glass with a sugar coated rim and the inside of the glass lined with a citrus rind

Cups A traditionally British category of wine based drinks

Daisy An oversized cocktail sweetened with fruit syrup served over crushed ice

Eggnog A blend of milk or cream, beaten eggs, sugar, and liquor, usually rum, brandy or whiskey and sometimes Sherry topped with nutmeg

Flip Cold creamy drinks made with eggs, sugar, alcohol and citrus juice

Highball A tall drink usually served with whiskey and ginger ale. The favorite drink of many drinkers' grandparents

Grog A rum based drink made with fruit and sugar

Julip A tall sweet drink usually made with Bourbon, water, sugar, crushed ice and occasionally mint. The most popular Julip being, of course, the Kentucky Derby's famous Mint Julip

Puff Made with equal parts alcohol and milk topped with club soda

Pousse-Café A drink made of layers created by floating liqueur according to their density (see page 29 on Pousse-Café cocktails and the accompanying density chart)

Rickey A cocktail made of alcohol (usually whisky, lime juice and soda water)

Sling A tall drink made with lemon juice, sugar and topped with club soda

Smash A short Julip

Toddy Served hot, it's a mixture of alcohol, spices and hot water

The following are more recent and popular drinks:

Blended Drinks Blender drinks consisting of ice, ice cream and a variety of other ingredients blended to a smooth though thick consistency

Cream Any drink made with ice cream, heavy cream, half and half or any of the famous bottled cream drinks

Mist Any type of alcoholic beverage served over crushed ice

Mojita A Cuban born drink prepared with sugar, muddled mint leaves, fresh lime juice, rum, ice, soda water, and garnished with mint leaves

Shooter A straight shot of alcohol, also sometimes called serving a drink "neat"

Sours Drinks made with lemon juice, sugar and alcohol

The next two types of drinks are new on the scene and sure to be filling the glasses of those in the know at a bar near you:

Stixx Tall muddled cocktails using different sized muddlers from 6 inches to 12 inches. Now they are muddling herbs, fruits, spices and a variety of ethnic and regional ingredients including beans, roots and spices.

Toppers Blended drinks with ice cream or crushed ice, the thicker the better, which is why these drinks are served with a spoon and a straw. They are made using cordials, flavored rums, flavored vodkas, blended fresh fruits and tropical juices. They are topped with crushed candy, fruits, nuts, and just about anything you can eat with a spoon.

Home Bar Recommendations & Tips

Location

Choosing the proper location is essential. Select an open area that is easily accessible. A kitchen counter or a sturdy table near the kitchen counter is well suited. It should be convenient to the refrigerator and sink. The kitchen also becomes a gathering point for many partiers. Cleaning up water and spills is a lot easier on your kitchen floor, than your carpet.

If your kitchen is too small, a location near your kitchen on a sturdy table and, if you're worried about your carpet, spread a small rug beneath.

When setting up for a party of 25 or more, it's best to use the diagram below known as the "Diamond Plan."

The "Diamond Plan" gives the best guest flow and has two focal points: food and liquor.

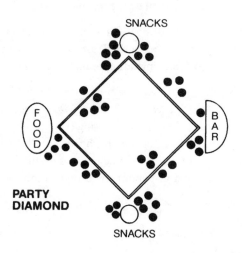

Stocking The Bar For Home

The traditional bartender's formula for setting up a simple home bar is:

— Something white (Vodka, Gin, Rum or Tequila)

— Something brown (Scotch, Canadian Whiskey or Bourbon)

— Something sweet (a Liqueur)

— Wine and/or Vermouth if you want an aperitif or plan on making martinis.

In stocking your home bar for the first time, don't attempt to buy all types of exotic liquors and liqueurs. Your inventory should be based on items you and your friends will use most. Keep in mind that people will bring their favorite brands as gifts.

We're into 2003 and premium liquor is the call. Folks might be drinking less, but they're drinking the best. Buy the best. It's only pennies more and saves a lot of excuses and embarrassment. Treat yourself and your guests to the best!!

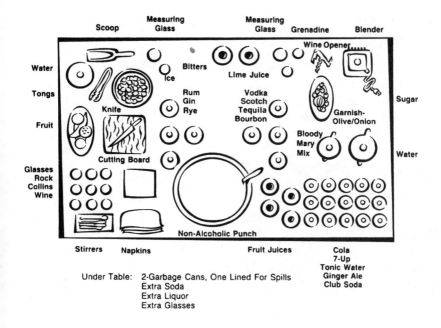

35

BASIC BAR STOCK AND PARTY TABLE

Product	Basic Stock (Quantities in Liters)	Number of Guests			
		10/30	30/40	40/60	60/100
White Wine					
Domestic (750 ml.)	2	4	4	6	8
Imported (750 ml.)	1	2	2	2	3
Red Wine					
Domestic (750 ml.)	2	1	2	3	3
Imported (750 ml.)	1	1	1	2	2
Blush Wine	1	1	2	2	2
Champagne					
Domestic (750 ml.)	1	2	3	4	4
Imported (750 ml.)	1	2	2	2	2
(Martini & Rossi Asti)					
Vermouth – Martini & Rossi					
Extra Dry (750 ml.)	1	1	1	2	2
Rosso (Sweet) (750 ml.)	1	1	1	1	1
Liquors					
Vodka – Vox	1	2	3	3	4
Rum – Bacardi	1	1	2	2	2
Gin – Bombay	1	1	2	2	3
Scotch – Dewars	1	1	2	2	3
Whiskey (choice of American/Canadian)	1	1	1	2	2
Bourbon – Knob Creek	1	1	1	1	1
Irish Whiskey – Tullamore Dew	1	1	1	1	2
Tequila – Jose Cuervo	1	2	2	2	3
Cognac – Hennessy	1	1	2	2	3
Beer (12 oz. bottles)	6	48	72	72	96
Others					
Aperitifs: (choice of 1)					
Campari	750 ml.	1	1	2	2
Dubonnet					
Red	750 ml.	1	1	1	2
Blonde	750 ml.	1	1	1	2
Lillet	750 ml.	1	1	1	2

BASIC BAR STOCK AND PARTY TABLE

Product	Basic Stock (Quantities in Liters)	Number of Guests			
		10/30	30/40	40/60	60/100
Cordials/Specials (choice of 3)					
Chambord	750 ml.	1	2	2	2
Cointreau	750 ml.	1	1	1	1
DeKuyper – Creme de Menthe White or Green	750 ml.	1	1	1	1
DeKuyper Peachtree Schnapps	750 ml.	1	1	1	1
DeKuyper Coffee Liqueur	750 ml.	1	1	1	1
DeKuyper – Creme de Cacao White or Dark	750 ml.	1	1	1	1
Carolans Irish Cream	750 ml.	1	2	3	3
DeKuyper Anisette or Sambuca	750 ml.	1	2	3	3
Disaronno Amaretto	750 ml.	1	2	2	2
Irish Mist	750 ml.	1	1	1	1
Drambuie	750 ml.	1	1	1	1

Number of Guests:	10/30	30/40	40/60	60/100
Cost (approximate):	$350-500	$500-600	$650-750	$750-900

---

1. This chart is based on $1\frac{3}{4}$ oz. per drink; this is a basic.

2. Product will vary on age (usually the younger the crowd, 21-35, the more beer and mixed drinks); so increase by one-half the amount of vodka, rum, tequila, and beer.

3. Geographical location is also important in selecting and cost of your liquor stock for your guests. Consult your local bartender or liquor clerk to find the most popular products in your area.

4. The time of the year or season should also be considered — in fall/winter less beer; spring serve more beer, rum, vodka, gin and tequila.

Other Supplies

Product	Basic Stock (Quantities in Liters)	Number of Guests			
		10/30	30/40	40/60	60/100
Soda (2 Liters):					
Club/Seltzer	1	3	3	4	5
Ginger Ale	1	2	2	2	3
Cola	1	3	3	3	4
Diet Cola	1	3	3	3	4
7-Up	1	2	3	3	4
Tonic	1	2	2	3	3
Juice (Quart):					
Tomato	1	2	2	3	3
Grapefruit	1	2	2	3	3
Orange	1	2	2	3	3
Cranberry	1	2	2	3	3
Miscellaneous:					
Ice (trays)	2	10	15	20	30
Napkins (dozen)	1	4	4	6	8
Stirrers (1,000/box)	1	1	1	1	1
Rose's Grenadine	1	1	1	1	2
Superfine Sugar (box)	1	1	1	1	1

Other Miscellaneous:

1 Quart Milk

2 Large Bottles Mineral Water

2 Bottles Rose's Lime Juice

1 Bottle Angostura Bitters

1 Bottle Worcestershire Sauce

1 Bottle McIlhenny Tabasco sauce

1 Small Jar Horseradish for Bloody Marys

1 Can Coco Lopez Cream of Coconut

Cocktail Recipes

A.C. C.

½ oz. Amaretto (Disaronno)

½ oz. Carolans Irish Cream

½ oz. Cointreau

Build.

A MIDSUMMER NIGHT'S DREAM

1½ oz. Jose Cuervo Especial

2½ oz. Pineapple juice

½ oz. Lemonade

½ oz. Rose's Grenadine

A TINKER TALL

1¼ oz. Irish Mist

3 oz. Ginger Ale

3 oz. Club Soda

Combine ingredients with lots of ice in a tall glass.

A-BOMB

½ oz. Vox Vodka

½ oz. DeKuyper Coffee Liqueur

½ oz. Carolans Irish Cream

½ oz. Cointreau

Shake with ice, strain, and serve in a highball glass.

A-BOMB II

½ oz. Carolans Irish Cream

½ oz. DeKuyper Coffee Liqueur

½ oz. Vox Vodka

Shake with ice and strain. You can also serve this one in a rocks glass.

ACAPULCO COCKTAIL

1 oz. Jose Cuervo Tequila

2 oz. Champagne

½ oz. Lime Juice

Sugar to taste. Stir gently.

ACAPULCO GOLD

1¼ oz. Jose Cuervo Especial Tequila

⅝ oz. Cointreau

1 oz. Sweet & Sour Mix

Blend with ice.

AFTER 5

1 part Carolans Irish Cream

1 part DeKuyper Peppermint Schnapps

Pour the ingredients in a shot glass.

AFTER 8

½ oz. Carolans Irish Cream

½ oz. DeKuyper Coffee Liqueur

½ oz. DeKuyper Green Créme de Menthe

Shake with ice. Strain into a shot glass.

AFTER DINNER MINT

1½ oz. DeKuyper Dark Creme de Cacao

½ oz. Carolans Irish Cream

2 drops DeKuyper Green Créme de Menthe

Layer liquors in the order they are given. Serve in a shooter glass.

AFTER
FIVE

1 oz. Carolans Irish
Cream

1 oz. DeKuyper
Peppermint
Schnapps

½ oz. DeKuyper Coffee
Liqueur

Shake with ice and strain into
shot glass.

ALABAMA
SLAMMER

1 part Disaronno Amaretto

1 part DeKuyper Sloe Gin

1 part Southern Comfort

splash Sweet & Sour mix

Shake with ice and strain into
shot glass.

ALAMO
SPLASH

1½ oz. Jose Cuervo Gold
Tequila

1 oz. Orange Juice

½ oz. Pineapple Juice

splash 7-Up

Mix well with cracked ice.
Strain and serve.

ALARM
CLOCK

1 oz. Drambuie

½ oz. Bacardi Dark Rum

½ oz. Knob Creek
Bourbon

Shake with ice and strain.

42

ALBUQUERQUE RÉAL

1½ oz. Jose Cuervo Especial Tequila

½ oz. Sweet & Sour Mix

¼ oz. Cranberry Juice

¼ oz. Cointreau

Stir all but Cointreau in the glass. Float the Cointreau. Serve in a cocktail glass.

ALEXANDER'S SISTER

1½ oz. Hennessy Cognac

1 oz. DeKuyper White Crème de Menthe

1 oz. Heavy cream/ice cream

Shake or blend and pour into a chilled cocktail glass.

ALGONQUIN

2 oz. Knob Creek Bourbon

½ oz. Martini & Rossi Dry Vermouth

1 oz. Pineapple Juice

Combine all ingredients in a shaker and shake. Strain into chilled cocktail glass.

ALLEGHENY

1¾ oz. Knob Creek Bourbon

½ oz. Martini & Rossi Dry Vermouth

1½ tsp. DeKuyper Blackberry-flavored Brandy

1½ tsp. Lemon Juice

Shake with ice and strain into cocktail glass. Add a twist of lemon peel on top.

ALL THAT RAZZ

2 oz. Bacardi Razz

1 oz. DeKuyper Peachtree
Schnapps

splash Cranberry juice

splash Pineapple juice

Shake and serve on the rocks.

Patrick
Funky Buddha
Chicago, IL

ALLIANCE

1 oz. Bombay Sapphire
Gin

1 oz. Martini & Rossi Dry
Vermouth

2 dashes Akvavit

Shake with ice and strain into
a rocks glass over ice.

ALMOND JOY

1 oz. Disaronno Amaretto

1 oz. DeKuyper White
Creme de Cacao

2 oz. Light Cream

Shake all ingredients with ice,
strain into a cocktail glass, and
serve.

ALMOND JOY SHOOTER

1½ oz. Disaronno Amaretto

½ oz. DeKuyper Dark
Creme de Cacao

½ oz. Vox Vodka

½ oz. Cream

Shake with ice. Strain and
serve straight up in a shot
glass.

ALMOND LEMONADE

1¼ oz. Vox Vodka

¼ oz. Disaronno Amaretto

Lemonade

Shake with ice and strain into a shot glass.

ALOHA

1 oz. Vox Vodka

½ oz. DeKuyper Apricot Brandy

2 oz. Pineapple Juice

Shake with ice, serve in tall glass. Garnish with pineapple wedge.

AMARETTO CAFE

1½ oz. Disaronno Amaretto

Hot black coffee

Stir. Top with whipped cream.

AMBROSIA

1 oz. Laird's Applejack

1 oz. Brandy

¼ oz. Cointreau

¼ oz. Lemon Juice

Champagne

Shake the first four ingredients over ice and strain into a champagne flute. Fill with Champagne.

AMERICAN BEAUTY

1 oz. Hennessy Cognac

1 oz. Orange Juice

½ oz. Martini & Rossi Dry Vermouth

¼ tsp. DeKuyper White Crème de Menthe

1 tsp. Rose's Grenadine

½ oz. Tawny Port

Shake with ice and strain into cocktail glass. Float port.

AMERICAN DREAM

½ oz. Disaronno Amaretto

½ oz. DeKuyper Dark Creme de Cacao

½ oz. DeKuyper Hazelnut Liqueur

½ oz. DeKuyper Coffee Liqueur

Shake with ice. Strain and serve straight up in cocktail glass.

AMERICAN ROSE

1½ oz. Hennessy Cognac

1 tsp. Rose's Grenadine

½ fresh peach, peeled and mashed

dashes Pernod

Champagne

Mix all ingredients, except champagne, with ice in a shaker or blender and pour into a chilled wine goblet. Fill with champagne.

AMERICANO

1 oz. Martini & Rossi Rosso Vermouth

1 oz. Campari

Club soda

Build with ice in a highball glass. Top with Club Soda and a twist of lemon.

ANGEL'S KISS

1½ oz. Lime or lemon juice

½ oz. Orange juice

½ oz. Cointreau

Soda water

Pour lime (or lemon juice), orange juice and Cointreau into a tumbler full of ice. Fill with soda water.

ANGEL'S DELIGHT

1 part Rose's Grenadine

1 part Cointreau

1 part DeKuyper Sloe Gin

1 part Heavy Cream

Layer this drink in the order listed. Start with grenadine on the bottom and finish with cream on top.

ANTI-FREEZE

1½ oz. Vox Vodka

½ oz. DeKuyper Melon Liqueur

Shake with ice, strain, and serve. You can also serve this one in a rocks glass.

APPARENT

¼ oz. Bombay Sapphire Gin

¼ oz. DeKuyper Light Creme de Cacao

Shake. Serve over rocks.

APPLE BLOSSOM

¾ oz. DeKuyper Sour Apple Pucker

¾ oz. Soda water

Serve on the rocks.

APPLE CRANBERRY SPRITZER

1 oz. DeKuyper Sour Apple Pucker

½ oz. Vox Vodka

4 oz. 7-Up

1½ oz. Cranberry juice

Serve on the rocks.

APPLE CRUSH

1½ oz. DeKuyper Sour Apple Pucker

dash Lime juice

Fill glass with ice and club soda.

APPLE DAIQUIRI

1 oz. Bacardi Rum

½ oz. DeKuyper Sour Apple Pucker

1 oz. Sweet & Sour Mix

2 wedge Cored apple

1 oz. Apple juice

Blend with ice and serve with an apple slice garnish.

APPLE FIZZ

1 oz. DeKuyper Sour Apple Pucker

½ oz. DeKuyper San Tropique

splash 7-Up

Add ice, fill with sweet & sour mix.

APPLE JACK

¾ oz. DeKuyper Sour Apple Pucker

¾ oz. Knob Creek Bourbon

Stir and serve over ice.

APPLEJACK STINGER

2 oz. Laird's Applejack

1 oz. DeKuyper White Creme de Menthe

Shake well with ice and strain into cocktail glass or over ice.

APPLE KIR

1 oz. Jose Cuervo Gold Tequila

½ oz. DeKuyper Crème de Cassis

1 oz. Apple Juice

1 tsp. Fresh Lemon Juice

Mix in a rocks glass over ice. Garnish with a Lemon Wedge.

APPLE LEMONADE

1 Lemon squeezed

1¼ oz. DeKuyper Sour
Apple Pucker

¾ oz. Vox Vodka

½ oz. Sugar water

1 oz. Sweet & sour mix

Top with 7-Up, garnish with
lemon and apple wedge.

APPLE MARGARITA

1¼ oz. DeKuyper Sour
Apple Pucker

¾ oz. Jose Cuervo Tequila

¾ oz. Lime juice

2 oz. Sweet & sour mix

Shake with ice and serve.

APPLE PIE

½ oz. DeKuyper Sour
Apple Pucker

½ oz. DeKuyper Hot
Damn!

Serve over ice.

APPLE PIE
A LA MODE

1 oz. DeKuyper Sour
Apple Pucker

½ oz. DeKuyper Hot
Damn!

2 scoops Vanilla ice cream

2 wedge Cored apple

2 dash Cinnamon powder

2 oz. Apple juice

Blend with ice and serve.
Garnish with an apple slice.

APPLE PIÑA
COLADA

¾ oz. Bacardi Rum

¾ oz. DeKuyper Sour
Apple Pucker

3 oz. Piña colada mix

Blend and serve.

APPLE PUCKERITA

¾ oz. Jose Cuervo Tequila

½ oz. DeKuyper Sour
Apple Pucker

Sweet & sour mix

dash Lime juice

Shake with ice, serve in a tall glass.

APPLE RUM FIZZ

1¼ oz. DeKuyper Sour
Apple Pucker

¾ oz. Bacardi Rum

½ oz. Rose's Grenadine

2 oz. Sweet & sour mix

Top with 7-Up.

APPLE SOUR

1¼ oz. DeKuyper Sour
Apple Pucker

3¼ oz. Sweet & sour mix

Shake with ice and serve.

APPLE SPAZZ

¾ oz. DeKuyper Sour
Apple Pucker

1 oz. DeKuyper
Razzmatazz

2 oz. Sweet & sour mix

Top with 7-Up.

APPLE STONE SOUR

1¼ oz. DeKuyper Sour
Apple Pucker

3¼ oz. Sweet & sour mix

Top with orange juice.

APPLE TAZZ

¾ oz. DeKuyper Sour
Apple Pucker

½ oz. DeKuyper
Razzmatazz

¾ oz. Vox Vodka

2 oz. Sweet & sour mix

Top with 7-Up.

APPLE TAZZ TEA

½ oz. DeKuyper Sour Apple Pucker

½ oz. DeKuyper Razzmatazz

½ oz. Vox Vodka

½ oz. Cointreau

2 oz. Sweet & sour mix

Top with cranberry juice.

APPLE VANILLA POP

DeKuyper Thrilla Vanilla

Blend with DeKuyper Sour Apple Pucker.

APPLE-ADE

2 parts DeKuyper Sour Apple Pucker

1 part Vox Vodka

Pour over ice in a tall glass. Fill with lemonade.

APPLE-BERRY PUCKER

Equal parts: DeKuyper Cheri-Beri and DeKuyper Sour Apple Pucker; or DeKuyper Sour Apple Pucker and cranberry juice.

APPLE-CRANBERRY SPRITZER

1 oz. DeKuyper Sour Apple Pucker

½ oz. Vox Vodka

4 oz. 7-Up

1½ oz. Cranberry juice

Serve in a tall glass with ice.

APPLETINI

1 part DeKuyper Sour Apple Pucker

1 part Vox Vodka

Served chilled in a martini glass. Garnish with an apple slice.

APRICOT ALEXANDER

1 oz. DeKuyper Apricot
        Flavored Brandy

1 oz. DeKuyper White
        Creme de Cacao

4 oz. Vanilla Ice Cream

Mix in blender until smooth.
Pour into wine glass.

APRICOT SOUR

2 tbsp. Lemon Juice

½ tsp. Superfine Sugar

2 oz. DeKuyper Apricot
        Brandy

3-4 Ice Cubes

Combine all ingredients in a
shaker and shake vigorously.
Strain into a chilled cocktail
glass. Garnish with Orange
slice and a Maraschino cherry.

APRICOT SOURBALL

1½ oz. DeKuyper Apricot
          Flavored Brandy

Juice ½ Lemon

Juice ½ Orange

In an on-the-rocks glass with
ice, top with lemon and
orange juices.

AQUATINI

1 part DeKuyper Island
          Blue Pucker

1 part Vox Vodka

Served chilled in a martini
glass with a lemon twist.

ARMORED CAR

1 oz. Disaronno Amaretto

1 oz. Jose Cuervo Tequila

Pour over ice in a rocks glass.
Garnish with a lime slice.

ASTI COSMO

Combine 1 oz. Cranberry juice, ¼ oz. Rose's Lime Juice and a splash of Cointreau in a chilled shaker and strain into a martini glass. Top with Martini & Rossi Asti.

ASTI SOUR

Combine 1½ oz. Disaronno Originale Amaretto and 2 oz. Sour mix in a chilled shaker and strain into a highball glass. Top with Martini & Rossi Asti and garnish with an orange slice or cherry.

ASTI HONEYDEW

Combine 1½ oz. DeKuyper Melon Liqueur and 3 oz. lemonade in a chilled shaker and strain into a highball glass. Top with Martini & Rossi Asti.

ASTI KIR

Pour 1 oz. DeKuyper Crème de Cassis into a 6 oz. flute and gently top with 5 oz. Martini & Rossi Asti.

ATOMIC GREEN

¼ oz.   DeKuyper Creme de Banana

½ oz.   DeKuyper Melon Liqueur

½ oz.   DeKuyper Peachtree Schnapps

½ oz.   Vox Vodka

1 oz.   Cream

Shake with ice. Strain and serve straight up.

AUNT ROSE

1¼ oz.   Irish Mist

2 oz.   Cranberry Juice

2 oz.   Orange Juice

Shake. Serve in a tall glass with ice.

AUNT TILLIE'S APPLE TEA

Brew a nice cup of tea and top liberally with Laird's Applejack. Squeeze in a wedge of lemon.

AVALANCHE

1½ oz. Carolans Irish Cream Liqueur, splash cold milk, 1 scoop vanilla ice cream. Blend.

AZUL LEMONADE

1¼ parts DeKuyper Island Blue Pucker

1 Lemon squeezed

2 parts Sweet and sour mix

1 Sugar packet

Served over ice and garnish with a lemon twist.

B&B COFFEE

1¼ oz. B&B Liqueur

4 oz. Hot coffee

Top with whipped cream.

B&B

1 oz. Benedictine

1 oz. Brandy

Stir and serve in a snifter.

B-52 WITH BOMBAY DOORS

1 part DeKuyper Coffee Liqueur

1 part Carolans Irish Cream

1 part Cointreau

1 part Bombay Sapphire Gin

Shake with ice and strain into a shot glass.

B52

1 oz. DeKuyper Coffee Liqueur

1 oz. Carolans Irish Cream

1 oz. Cointreau

Layer Coffee Liqueur, Carolans and Cointreau into a large shot glass.

BABY BABY

2 oz. Orange juice

1 oz. Vox Vodka

1 oz. Cointreau

Pour orange juice, Vox Vodka and Cointreau into a tumbler glass with ice. Stir.

BACARDI & COLA

1½ oz. Bacardi Light or Dark Rum

3 oz. Cola

Pour Rum into tall glass filled with ice. Fill with your favorite Cola and garnish with a squeeze of a Lemon.

BACARDI & TONIC

1¼ oz. Bacardi Light Rum

Tonic

Pour Rum into a tall glass filled with ice. Fill with Tonic.

BACARDI BLOSSOM

1¼ oz. Bacardi Light Rum

1 oz. Orange Juice

½ oz. Lemon Juice

½ tsp. Sugar

Blend with crushed ice and pour. Garnish with a spring flower.

BACARDI GINGER-N-SPICE

1½ oz. Bacardi Spice Rum

Ginger Ale

In a tall glass with ice, add rum and fill with Ginger Ale.

BACARDI BUCK

1¼ oz. Bacardi Light or
      Añejo Rum

Ginger Ale

Pour rum in highball glass
filled with ice. Add Ginger Ale
and garnish with twist of
lemon peel.

BACARDI CHAMPAGNE COCKTAIL

1 oz. Bacardi Select Rum

Champagne

1 tsp. Sugar

dash Bitters

In a tall glass, mix Rum,
Sugar and Bitters. Fill with
Champagne.

BACARDI COCKTAIL

1¼ oz. Bacardi Light Rum

1 oz. Rose's Lime Juice

½ tsp. Sugar

½ oz. Rose's Grenadine

Mix in a shaker with ice and
strain into a chilled cocktail
glass.

The New York Supreme Court
ruled in 1936 that a Bacardi
Cocktail is not a Bacardi
Cocktail unless it's made with
Bacardi Rum.

BACARDI COLLINS

2 oz. Bacardi Light Rum

2 tsp. Frozen lemonade or limeade concentrate

½ tsp. Sugar

Club Soda

Combine first two ingredients in a tall glass with ice. Fill with club soda.

BACARDI DAIQUIRI

1¼ oz. Bacardi Light Rum

½ oz. Lemon Juice

½ tsp. Sugar

Mix in shaker with ice and strain into a chilled cocktail glass.

BACARDI DRY MARTINI

2 oz. Bacardi Light Rum

½ oz. Martini & Rossi Dry Vermouth

Shake with ice and strain.

BACARDI FIRESIDE

1¼ oz. Bacardi Light or Dark Rum

1 tsp. Sugar

Hot Tea

In a mug, add Sugar and Rum. Fill with very Hot Tea and one Cinnamon Stick. Stir.

BACARDI FIZZ

1¼ oz. Bacardi Light Rum

¼ oz. Lemon juice

¼ oz. Rose's Grenadine

Club soda

Pour rum and lemon juice in a highball glass filled with ice. Add the grenadine and fill with club soda.

BACARDI HEMINGWAY

1½ oz. Bacardi Light Rum

Juice of ½ Lime

¼ oz. Grapefruit Juice

¼ oz. Maraschino Liqueur

Mix with ice and serve. Ernest Hemingway would have written about this one.

BACARDI HOT BUTTERED RUM

In a mug put 1 tsp. sugar, ½ tsp. butter, 1 jigger Bacardi light or dark rum, 4 cloves. Fill with boiling water. Stir.

BACARDI HOT COFFEE

1½ oz. Bacardi Light or Dark Rum to a cup of coffee. Whipped cream optional.

BACARDI LIMÓN COSMOPOLITAN

2 oz. Bacardi Limón

1 oz. Cointreau

½ oz. Lime juice

Cranberry juice

Garnish with lemon twist.

BACARDI LIMÓN MARTINI

2 oz. Bacardi Limón

dash Martini & Rossi Extra Dry Vermouth

splash Cranberry Juice

Stir in a cocktail glass. Garnish with Lemon.

It's a new twist on an old classic. First invented at the Heart and Soul in San Francisco, California.

BACARDI MARTINI COCKTAIL

1½ oz. Bacardi Rum

dash Martini & Rossi Extra Dry Vermouth

Add olive.

BACARDI MOJITO

1½ oz. Bacardi Light Rum

6 Mint leaves

½ Lime

2 dashes Angostura bitters

Club soda

In a collins glass, place mint leaves and lime. Crush well with the back of a spoon. Add bitters and sugar. Fill glass with ice. Add Rum and top with club soda. Stir well and garnish with sprig of mint or lime wheel.

BACARDI O COFFEE

2 oz. Bacardi O™

3 oz. Hot coffee

Serve in cup. Top with Carolans Irish Cream.

BACARDI O COFFEE II

2 oz. Bacardi O™

3 oz. Hot Coffee

splash Carolans Irish Cream

splash DeKuyper Green Creme de Menthe

Serve in a cup. Top with Carolans Irish Cream and Green Creme de Menthe.

BACARDI O TINI

1½ oz. Bacardi O™

¾ oz. Pineapple Juice

Shake; serve in a chilled glass; float Chambord.

BACARDI PINK SQUEEZE

1½ oz. Bacardi Light Rum

Pink lemonade

Pour Rum into tall glass filled with ice. Fill with Pink Lemonade.

BACARDI RUM CAPPUCCINO

1½ oz. Bacardi Dark Rum

Coffee

1 tsp. Sugar

Ground Cinnamon

Whipped Cream

Combine the Rum and Sugar in a glass. Add equal parts Hot Coffee and Milk. Top with Steamed Milk, Whipped Cream and Cinnamon.

BACARDI SPICE CARIBBEAN MARTINI

2½ oz. Bacardi Spice Rum

½ oz. DeKuyper Creme de Banana

Shake and strain. Serve up. Garnish with pineapple wedge.

BACARDI SUNSET

1¼ oz. Bacardi Light Rum

3 oz. Orange Juice

squeeze Lime

Combine in a tall glass with crushed ice. Add a squeeze of Lime. Garnish with an Orange Wheel.

What a way to end the day.

BACARDI SWEET MARTINI

2 oz. Bacardi Light Rum

½ oz. Martini & Rossi Rosso Vermouth

Stir gently with ice in a cocktail glass.

BACARDI TU TU CHERRY

1 oz. Bacardi Rum

¼ oz. DeKuyper Cherry Liqueur

2 oz. Orange juice

3 oz. Cranberry juice

Shake with ice.

BACARDI YEAH MARTINI COCKTAIL

$1\frac{1}{2}$ oz. Bacardi O™

$2\frac{1}{2}$ oz. Pineapple Juice

$1\frac{1}{2}$ oz. Cranberry Juice

splash Soda

Serve up in a chilled glass; garnish with a lime and maraschino cherry.

BACK IN BLACK

1 oz. Cointreau

$1\frac{1}{2}$ oz. Jose Cuervo Tequila

Cola

Pour Cointreau and Cuervo into a tumbler glass with ice. Fill with cola. Stir.

BACKDRAFT

1 oz. Drambuie

1 oz. Cointreau

Serve as a shot.

BAGPIPE

$1\frac{1}{4}$ oz. Dewar's Scotch

Hot Coffee

Top with whipped cream or ice cream.

BALALAÏKA

$\frac{1}{2}$ oz. Lemon juice

$\frac{1}{2}$ oz. Cointreau

$1\frac{1}{2}$ oz. Vox Vodka

Shake lemon juice, Cointreau and Vox Vodka with ice. Strain into a cocktail glass.

BAMBOO COCKTAIL

1½ oz. Sherry

¾ oz. Martini & Rossi Dry
        Vermouth

dash Angostura Bitters

Stir with ice and strain.

BANANA BOAT

¾ oz. Bacardi Rum

¾ oz. DeKuyper Creme de
        Banana Liqueur

¼ oz. Pineapple Juice

Serve in a tall glass.

BANANA DAIQUIRI

1¼ oz. Bacardi Light Rum

¼ oz. Lemon Juice or
        Rose's Lime Juice

½ tsp. Sugar

1 Banana, peeled

Blend.

BANANA MAN

1 oz. Bacardi Light Rum

¼ oz. DeKuyper Creme de
        Banana Liqueur

½ oz. Lemon Juice or
        Rose's Lime Juice

Blend with ice and serve.

BANANA MARTINI

2½ oz. Vox Vodka

splash DeKuyper Creme de
Banana

splash Martini & Rossi
Extra-dry Vermouth

Serve over ice with a banana
slice.

BANANA RUM CREAM

1½ oz. Bacardi Dark Rum

½ oz. DeKuyper Creme de
Banana

1 oz. Light Cream

Shake well. Serve straight up
or with ice.

BANANA SPLIT

DeKuyper Cheri-Beri Pucker
and DeKuyper Creme de
Banana mixed. Serve in a low-
ball glass with ice, garnished
with whipped cream, topped
with Maraschino cherry.

BANILLA BOAT

1 oz. Drambuie

½ oz. DeKuyper Creme de
Banana

4 oz. Vanilla Ice Cream

splash Chambord

Blend until smooth. Serve in a
champagne glass. Pour
Chambord over top. Garnish
with a banana slice.

BANSHEE

¾ oz. DeKuyper Creme de
Banana

¾ oz. DeKuyper Light
Creme de Cacao

3 oz. Cream

Blend with crushed ice. Serve
in tulip glass.

BARBERRY COAST

1¼ oz. Chambord

1½ oz. Cranberry Juice

½ oz. Grapefruit Juice

Serve over ice in tall glass.

BARN BURNER

1½ oz. Southern Comfort

small Stick cinnamon

slice Lemon peel

Hot cider

Put cinnamon, lemon peel, Southern Comfort in mug; fill with hot cider; stir.

BARRACUDA

1¼ oz. Bacardi Dark Rum

1 oz. Pineapple Juice

½ oz. Rose's Lime Juice

¼ tsp. Sugar

Champagne

Shake everything but the Champagne. Serve in a champagne glass and fill to the top with Champagne.

BASIN STREET

2 oz. Knob Creek Bourbon

½ oz. Cointreau

1 oz. Lemon Juice

Shake well with cracked ice and strain into cocktail glass.

BAY BREEZE

2 parts Vox Vodka

4 parts Cranberry juice

2 parts Pineapple juice

Shake ingredients with ice and strain into ice-filled glass.

BEACH PARTY

1¼ oz. Bacardi Light or Dark Rum

1 oz. Pineapple Juice

1 oz. Orange Juice

1 oz. Rose's Grenadine

Blend with ice.

BEACH BUM

1 oz. Vox Vodka

1½ oz. DeKuyper Melon Liqueur

1 oz. Cranberry Juice

Mix in a shaker with ice. Strain.

BEACHED WHALE

½ oz. Cointreau

½ oz. DeKuyper White Creme de Cacao

1 oz. Advocaat

Shake with ice, serve in rocks glass.

BEACH COMBER

1½ oz. Bacardi Light Rum

¾ oz. Rose's Lime Juice

¼ oz. Cointreau

dash Maraschino Liqueur

Shake. Serve straight up or with ice.

BEAM ME UP SCOTTY

Equal parts: Carolans Irish Cream Liqueur, DeKuyper Coffee Liqueur, DeKuyper Creme de Banana.

BEE'S KISS

1 oz. Bacardi Light Rum

¼ oz. Bacardi Dark Rum

¾ oz. Cream

2 bsp. Honey

Shake. Serve over ice.

BELGIAN COFFEE

Cointreau, Carolans Irish
Cream, hot coffee.

BELLINI EASY

1 oz. DeKuyper Peachtree
       Schnapps

3 oz. Champagne

Pour Schnapps in a
champagne glass and
add Champagne.

BELLINI TINI

Bacardi O™, peach nectar,
splash of orange juice, splash
of Champagne. Serve in glass
rim dipped in strawberry juice.

Butterfield 8
Chicago, IL

BELLISIMO MARTINI

1 oz. Disaronno Amaretto

1 oz. Bacardi O™

splash Cranberry Juice

Stir with ice and strain into a
martini glass.

BERI-BERI

Equal parts of

       DeKuyper
       Cheri-Beri Pucker

       Vox Vodka

Serve on the rocks.

BERMUDA ROSE

1 oz. Bombay Sapphire
Gin

¼ oz. DeKuyper Apricot
Flavored Brandy

½ oz. Rose's Lime Juice

dash Rose's Grenadine

Shake with ice and strain.

BETWEEN THE SHEETS

1 part Cointreau

1 part Hennessy Cognac

1 part Bacardi Light Rum

dash Lemon Juice

Shake with ice. Strain into a
sugar-rimmed glass.

BIG SLOPPY WET KISS

1 part DeKuyper
Cheri-Beri

1 part DeKuyper Sour
Apple Pucker

1 part DeKuyper Grape
Schnapps

splash Sweet & Sour Mix

Top with lemon-lime soda.

BIKINI MARTINI

2 oz. Bombay Sapphire
Gin

¼ oz. Freshly squeezed
lime juice

¼ oz. DeKuyper Blue
Curacao

¼ oz. DeKuyper Peachtree
Schnapps

Sugar syrup

Shake and strain into martini
glass.

BITCH ON WHEELS

¼ oz. Martini & Rossi
Extra Dry Vermouth

1 oz. Bombay Sapphire
Gin

¼ oz. Pernod

¼ oz. DeKuyper White
Crème de Menthe

Shake ingredients with ice and strain into a chilled cocktail glass.

*Invented at Stars
San Francisco, California*

BLACK BOMBAY SAPPHIRE GIN

1½ oz. Bombay Sapphire
Gin

½ oz. Black Sambuca

2 tsp. Martini & Rossi
Rosso Vermouth

Shake. Strain into a cocktail glass and serve.

BLACK BUCK

1¼ oz. Bacardi Dark Rum

Ginger Ale

Pour Rum in a tall glass with ice. Fill with Ginger Ale and garnish with Lemon.

BLACK DEVIL

1½ oz. Bacardi Light Rum

½ oz. Martini & Rossi Dry
Vermouth

1 Pitted Black Olive

Stir well with ice and strain into martini glass.

BLACK ICE

1 oz. Black Sambuca

1 oz. Vox Vodka

¼ oz. DeKuyper Crème de
Menthe

Shake with ice and strain. You can also serve this one over ice in a highball glass.

BLACK MAGIC

1½ oz. Vox Vodka

¾ oz. DeKuyper Coffee
Liqueur

dash Lemon Juice

Shake with cracked ice. Add a
dash of Lemon Juice.

BLACK ORCHID

1 oz. Vox Vodka

½ oz. DeKuyper Blue
Curacao

1½ oz. Cranberry Juice

Build over ice in a 7 oz. rocks
glass.

BLACK RUSSIAN

1½ oz. Vox Vodka

¾ oz. DeKuyper Coffee
Liqueur

Add Vox Vodka and then
DeKuyper Coffee Liqueur to a
glass filled with cubed ice. Stir
briskly. Garnish with a Swizzle
Stick. Add cream for a White
Russian.

BLACK SUN

½ oz. Bacardi Light Rum

Cola

1½ oz. Cointreau

Pour Bacardi and Cointreau
into tumbler glass with ice.
Fill with cola. Stir.

BLACK TARTAN

¼ oz. Drambuie

1 oz. Dewar's Scotch

¼ oz. Tullamore Dew Irish
Whiskey

¼ oz. DeKuyper Coffee
Liqueur

Shake. Serve over rocks.

BLACK TRUFFLE MARTINI

2 oz. Bombay Sapphire Gin

splash Martini & Rossi Extra Dry Vermouth

1 fresh Clean Black Truffle

Mix ingredients with cracked ice in shaker; strain into martini glass. Garnish with a small, fresh black truffle.

BLACK VELVET (A.K.A. BISMARCK OR CHAMPAGNE VELVET)

1 part Guinness Stout

1 part Champagne

Layer the Champagne over the Guinness in a champagne flute.

BLACKTHORN

1½ oz. Tullamore Dew Irish Whiskey

1½ oz. Martini & Rossi Dry Vermouth

3-4 dashes Pernod

3-4 dashes Angostura Bitters

Shake or blend with ice. Pour into a chilled rocks glass.

BLARNEY COCKTAIL

1½ oz. Tullamore Dew Irish Whiskey

1 oz. Martini & Rossi Dry Vermouth

splash DeKuyper Green Crème de Menthe

Shake well with ice. Strain into a cocktail glass. Serve with a Green Cherry.

BLARNEY STONE COCKTAIL

2 oz. Tullamore Dew Irish Whiskey

½ tsp. Pernod

½ tsp. Cointreau

¼ tsp. Rose's Grenadine

1 dash Angostura Bitters

Shake with ice and strain. Serve with a twist of Orange Peel and an Olive.

BLIGHTER BOB

1 oz. Bacardi Light Rum

½ oz. Bacardi Dark Rum

½ oz. DeKuyper Crème de Cassis

1 oz. Orange Juice

2 dashes Orange Bitters

2 oz. Ginger Ale

Stir and serve straight up or with ice. Garnish with a Lemon Twist.

BLIZZARD

1¼ oz. Vox Vodka

Fresca

In a tall glass with ice. Garnish with twist of lemon.

BLONDE MARTINI

Bombay Sapphire. Enlivened with Lillet Blonde.

Brasserie Jo Martini's Chicago, IL

BLOODY BULL

1¼ oz. Vox Vodka

2½ oz. Tomato Juice

1½ oz. Beef Bouillon

1-2 tsp. Lemon Juice

dash Worcestershire

dash Tabasco Sauce

dash Pepper

Combine with ice in a shaker. Strain into a coffee glass.

BLOODY CAESAR

1¼ oz. Vox Vodka

2½ oz. Clamato Juice

dash Worcestershire

dash Tabasco Sauce

dash Salt and Pepper

Pour Vox Vodka into a glass with ice and fill with Clamato Juice. Add a dash of Tabasco, Worcestershire, Pepper, and Salt. Garnish with a Celery Stalk or a Lime Wheel.

BLUE DIABLO

1 part Jose Cuervo Clásico

4 parts Lemon-Lime Soda

splash DeKuyper Blue Curacao

Combine Cuervo and lemon-lime soda in a rocks glass with ice. Add splash of Blue Curacao. Garnish with sugar on the rim.

BLUE HOOTER

1 part DeKuyper Island Blue Pucker

1 part DeKuyper Watermelon Pucker

Serve as a shot.

BLUE LADY

1 oz. Bombay Sapphire Gin

¼ oz. DeKuyper Blue Curacao

1 oz. Lemon Mix

Shake. Serve over ice.

BLUE LAGOON

1½ oz. Vox Vodka

½ oz. DeKuyper Blue Curacao

3 oz. Lemonade

Combine ingredients over ice in a highball glass.

BLUE LAGOON MARTINI

1¼ oz. Bacardi Limón

½ oz. DeKuyper Blue Curacao

¼ oz. Martini & Rossi Dry Vermouth

Garnish with strawberry or olives.

Alex Refojo
Club Mystique
Miami, FL

BLUE MONDAY

½ oz. Bombay Sapphire Gin

1½ oz. Cointreau

Soda water

Pour Bombay Sapphire Gin and Cointreau into a tumbler glass with ice. Fill with soda water. Add a drop of blue curacao. Stir.

BLUE RIBAND

1½ oz. Bombay Sapphire Gin

¼ oz. Cointreau

¼ oz. DeKuyper Blue Curacao

BLUE SHARK MARTINI

1½ oz. Vox Vodka

1½ oz. Jose Cuervo Tequila

½ oz. DeKuyper Blue Curacao

Shake and strain into martini glass or over ice.

BLUE VELVET

1 part Pucker Island Blue

1 part Vox Vodka

1 part Cointreau

splash Lime

splash Cranberry Juice

Garnish with lime wedge.

BLUEBERRY TEA

Cointreau, Disaronno
Amaretto and hot tea.
Garnished with an orange
slice.

BLUEBERRY SAPPHIRE

1 oz. Bombay Sapphire
Gin

1 oz. DeKuyper Blueberry
Schnapps

Mix ingredients with cracked
ice in shaker; strain into martini glass. Top with sour mix,
DeKuyper Blue Curacao (for
color) and blueberries.

*Served at Lola Bar
Los Angeles, CA*

BOBBY BURNS

1½ oz. Dewar's White Label

½ oz. Martini & Rossi
Rosso Vermouth

3 dashes Benedictine

A version of the classic Rob
Roy. Build in cocktail glass
over ice. Stir and serve.

BOCCI BALL

½ oz. Disaronno Amaretto

½ oz. Vox Vodka

½ oz. Orange Juice

Shake with ice. Serve straight
up in a shot glass.

You can also serve this one
over ice in a rocks glass.

BOILERMAKER

1¼ oz. Tullamore Dew Irish
Whiskey

10 oz. Beer

Serve whiskey in a shot glass
with a glass of beer.

BOMBAY CLOUD

2 oz. Bombay Sapphire
Gin

¼ oz. DeKuyper Apricot
Brandy

1 oz. Orange juice

Grenadine syrup

BOMBAY SAPPHIRE
GIN ALEXANDER

1 part Bombay Sapphire
Gin

1 part DeKuyper White
Creme de Cacao

3 parts Half & Half

Shake with ice and serve up or
on the rocks. Dust with nutmeg.

BOMBAY
SAPPHIRE GIN
AND CRAN

1¼ oz. Bombay Sapphire
Gin

2½ oz. Cranberry Juice

Serve on the rocks.

BOMBAY
SAPPHIRE GIN
AND PINK

2 oz. Bombay Sapphire
Gin

3 oz. Tonic water

dash Bitters

Lemon peel

Pour into tall glass with ice.
Lemon peel garnish.

BOMBAY SAPPHIRE GIN AND SIN

1¼ oz. Bombay Sapphire Gin

¼ oz. Orange Juice

¼ oz. Lemon Juice

2 dashes Grenadine

Shake Bombay, orange juice, lemon juice and grenadine with ice. Strain into a chilled cocktail glass.

BOMBAY SAPPHIRE GIN AND TONIC

2 oz. Bombay Sapphire Gin

3 oz. Tonic

In a tall glass filled with ice, add Bombay and fill with tonic. Add squeeze of lime.

BOMBAY SAPPHIRE GIN APPLE TONIC

1 part Bombay Sapphire Gin

1½ parts DeKuyper Sour Apple Pucker

Pour over ice in a tall glass. Fill with tonic.

BOMBAY SAPPHIRE GIN CASSIS

3 parts Bombay Sapphire Gin

1 part DeKuyper Creme de Cassis

Stir on the rocks.

BOMBAY SAPPHIRE GIN COCKTAIL AKA DUBONNET COCKTAIL

1 part Bombay Sapphire Gin

2 parts Dubonnet

Stir on the rocks. Add lemon twist.

BOMBAY SAPPHIRE GIN DRIVER

1¼ oz. Bombay Sapphire
        Gin

4 oz. Orange Juice

       Tonic Water

In a tall glass filled with ice.

BOMBAY SAPPHIRE GIN FIZZ

2 oz. Bombay Sapphire
       Gin

1 tsp. Sugar

        Juice of 1 Lemon

        Club Soda

Shake first three ingredients
with ice and strain. Fill with
Club Soda.

BOMBAY SAPPHIRE GINGER COLADA

1½ oz. Coco Lopez
        Cream of Coconut

1 oz. Canton Delicate
       Ginger Liqueur

½ oz. Bombay Sapphire
       Gin

½ oz. Bacardi Rum

Blend.

BOMBAY SAPPHIRE GIN JULEP

1¼ oz. Bombay Sapphire
        Gin

4 Sprigs Mint

1 tsp. Sugar

In a highball glass filled with
shaved ice, stir until glass is
frosted. Garnish with fresh
mint.

BOMBAY SAPPHIRE GINOLANS

2 parts Carolans Irish
          Cream

1 part Bombay Sapphire
         Gin

Stir.

BOMBAY SAPPHIRE GIN OLD FASHIONED

$1\frac{1}{4}$ oz. Bombay Sapphire
         Gin

2 dashes Bitters

$\frac{1}{4}$ tsp. Sugar

        Club Soda

Crush (muddle) orange slice, bitters and cherry on bottom of rocks glass. Add ingredients, fill with ice and club soda.

BOMBAY SAPPHIRE GIN RICKEY

$1\frac{1}{4}$ oz. Bombay Sapphire
         Gin

        Club Soda

In a tall glass filled with ice, add Bombay and fill with club soda. Add squeeze of lime.

BOMBAY SAPPHIRE GIN SCREWDRIVER

$1\frac{1}{4}$ oz. Bombay Sapphire
         Gin

        Orange Juice

In a tall glass filled with ice, add Bombay and fill with orange juice.

BOMBAY SAPPHIRE MARTINI

1½ oz. Bombay Sapphire Gin

dash Martini & Rossi Extra Dry Vermouth

Shake with ice. Strain and serve straight up or on the rocks with some ice in cocktail glass. Add lemon twist or olive.

BONBINI

1 oz. Bacardi Light or Dark Rum

¼ oz. DeKuyper Orange Curacao

dash Bitters

Stir and serve with ice.

BOOTLEGGER MARTINI

2 oz. Bombay Sapphire Gin

¼ oz. Southern Comfort

Stir gently with ice; serve straight up or over ice. Garnish with a Lemon Twist.

Chianti Restaurant Houston, Texas

BOSTON BREEZE

1 oz. Coco Lopez Cream of Coconut

1¼ oz. Bacardi Rum

3 oz. Cranberry Juice

1 cup Ice

Blend and serve in a margarita glass.

BOURBON AND WATER

2 oz. Knob Creek Bourbon

2½ oz. Water

Pour Bourbon and water into old-fashioned glass. Add ice and a twist of lemon peel, if desired, and stir.

BOURBON HIGHBALL

2 oz. Knob Creek Bourbon

3 oz. Ginger Ale or Club Soda

Fill highball glass with Bourbon, ginger ale or club soda, and ice cubes. Add twist of lemon peel, if desired, and stir.

BOURBON ON THE ROCKS

2 oz. Knob Creek Bourbon

Pour over ice slowly.

BOW STREET SPECIAL

1½ oz. Tullamore Dew Irish Whiskey

¾ oz. Cointreau

1 oz. Lemon Juice

Shake or blend and strain into a chilled cocktail glass.

BRAIN HEMORRHAGE

3 parts Carolans Irish
Cream

1 part DeKuyper
Peachtree Schnapps

dash Rose's Grenadine

Combine in a shot glass.

BRAINSTORM

1¾ oz. Tullamore Dew Irish
Whiskey

¼ oz. Martini & Rossi Dry
Vermouth

dash Benedictine

Stir all ingredients and strain
into a cocktail glass. Decorate
with a twist of Orange Peel.

BRANDY ALEXANDER

1½ oz. Brandy or Hennessy
Cognac

½ oz. DeKuyper Dark
Crème de Cacao

1 oz. Sweet Cream or
Ice Cream

Shake or blend with ice. Strain.

BRANDY EGGNOG

2-3 oz. Hennessy Cognac

½ oz. Superfine sugar or
to taste

1 cup Milk

1 Beaten egg

Freshly ground
nutmeg

Shake with ice or blend and
strain into a chilled martini
glass or cup. Sprinkle with
nutmeg.

BRANDY FIX

2-3 oz. Hennessy Cognac

1 tsp. Sugar

1 tsp. Water

Juice of ½ lemon

Pour into an Old Fashioned glass and fill with ice. Stir.

BRANDY FIZZ

2-3 oz. Hennessy Cognac

1½ oz. Lemon juice or half lime and lemon juice

½ oz. Sugar syrup or to taste

Club soda

Shake and pour into a highball glass, fill with club soda.

BRASS KNUCKLE

1 oz. Knob Creek Bourbon

½ oz. Cointreau

2 oz. Sweetened Lemon Mix

Shake with ice and serve in a highball glass with ice.

BRAVE BULL

1½ oz. Jose Cuervo Tequila

½ oz. DeKuyper Coffee Liqueur

Stir and serve over ice.

BRAVO

1 oz. Vox Vodka

½ oz. Campari

Pour Vox Vodka and Campari over ice in a tall glass. Top with tonic. Garnish with slice of lemon and lime.

BREAKFAST MARTINI

2 oz. Bombay Sapphire Gin

⅛ oz. Martini and Rossi Extra Dry Vermouth

½ oz. Freshly squeezed lemon juice

⅛ tsp. Orange marmalade

Orange peel garnish.

BRONX COCKTAIL

½ oz. Bombay Sapphire Gin

2 tsp. Martini & Rossi Extra Dry Vermouth

2 tsp. Martini & Rossi Rosso Vermouth

2 oz. Orange Juice

Shake with ice. Serve over rocks.

BUBBLE GUM

½ oz. DeKuyper Melon Liqueur

½ oz. Vox Vodka

½ oz. DeKuyper Crème de Banana

½ oz. Orange Juice

dash Rose's Grenadine

Serve in a shot glass.

BUCK-A-ROO

1¼ oz. Bacardi Light or Dark Rum

Root Beer

Pour Rum into a collins glass filled with ice. Fill with Root Beer.

BUCKING IRISH

1¼ oz. Tullamore Dew Irish Whiskey

5 oz. Ginger Ale

Combine in an ice-filled collins glass. Garnish with a Lemon Twist.

BULL AND BEAR

1¾ oz. Knob Creek
        Bourbon

¾ oz. Cointreau

1 Tbs. Rose's Grenadine

Juice of ½ Lime

Shake with cracked ice.
Garnish with maraschino
cherry and orange slice.

BULLSHOT

1½ oz. Vox Vodka

1 tsp. Lemon Juice

dash Worcestershire

dash Tabasco

4 oz. Chilled Beef
       Bouillon

dash Salt and Pepper

Shake and serve in a glass.
Garnish with a Lemon Wedge.

BUNGI JUMPER

1¼ oz. Irish Mist

4 oz. Orange juice

½ oz. Cream

splash Disaronno Amaretto

Mix all but the Amaretto in
a highball glass. Float the
Disaronno Amaretto on top.

BURNT RAYBIRD

½ oz. Disaronno Amaretto

½ oz. DeKuyper Dark
       Creme de Cacao

½ oz. DeKuyper Coffee
       Liqueur

Hot coffee

Pour into coffee mug.

BUSHRANGER

1 oz. Dubonnet

1 oz. Bacardi Light Rum

2 dashes Angostura Bitters

Stir and serve over ice.

BUSHWACKER

2 oz. Coco Lopez Cream of Coconut

2 oz. Half & Half

1 oz. DeKuyper Coffee Liqueur

½ oz. DeKuyper Dark Crème de Cacao

½ oz. Bacardi Rum

1 cup Ice

Blend and serve in a margarita glass.

BUTTERSCOTCH COLLINS

½ oz. Drambuie

1 tsp. Sugar

Water

1½ oz. Dewar's Scotch

2 oz. Lemon Juice

1 oz. Soda

Dissolve sugar in water. Pour over ice in collins glass. Add Dewar's, Drambuie and lemon juice. Stir, top with soda. Garnish with a Maraschino cherry and orange slice.

BUTTERY NIPPLE

⅓ oz. Carolans Irish Cream

⅓ oz. Vox Vodka

⅓ oz. DeKuyper Butterscotch Schnapps

Combine in a shot glass.

CAFE AMARETTO

1 oz. Disaronno Amaretto

½ oz. DeKuyper Coffee Liqueur

Coffee

Pour into a mug or coffee cup.

CAFE CACAO

2 oz. DeKuyper Creme de Cacao

Coffee

Topped with Whipped Cream.

CAFE CARIBBEAN

1 oz. Disaronno Amaretto

1 oz. Bacardi Rum

3 oz. Coffee

Sugar to taste

Pour into coffee cup or mug.

CAFE DISARONNO

Pour 1½ oz. Disaronno
Amaretto into a coffee cup.
Fill with hot coffee. Garnish
with whipped cream and a
sprinkling of cinnamon.

CAFE ITALIA

1½ oz. Disaronno Amaretto

Hennessy Cognac

Fill with coffee. Top with
whipped cream.

CAFE MEXICANO

1 oz. DeKuyper Coffee
Liqueur

½ oz. Jose Cuervo Tequila

Hot Coffee

Top with whipped cream.

CAIPIRINHA DE FRANCIA

½ Glass limes,
muddled

¾ oz. Sugar syrup

2 oz. Bacardi Light Rum

Serve in a tall glass.

CALIFORNIA COOLAID

1¼ oz. Bacardi Light or
Añejo Rum

Orange juice

Milk

Pour Bacardi into a tall glass
half filled with ice. Add half
orange juice and half milk.
Stir.

CAMERON'S KICK

¾ oz. Tullamore Dew Irish
Whiskey

¾ oz. Dewar's Scotch
Whisky

Juice of ¼ Lemon

2 dashes Angostura Bitters

Shake well with cracked ice
and strain into a cocktail
glass.

CAMPARI ORANGE

⅓ Campari

⅔ Orange juice

Ice cubes

Put ice in glass. Add orange
juice and Campari. Stir and
serve.

CAMPARTINI

2 oz. Campari

2 oz. Vox Vodka

dash Rose's Lime Juice

splash Orange Juice

Shake, serve with orange slice
in tall glass.

CANADIAN COFFEE

½ oz. Canadian Club

½ oz. DeKuyper Coffee Liqueur

½ oz. Disaronno Amaretto

Hot coffee

Top with whipped cream and a maraschino cherry.

CANDY ASS

1 oz. Chambord

1 oz. DeKuyper Chocolate Liqueur

Shake with ice and strain into a shot glass.

CANTON SUNRISE

1½ oz. Canton Delicate Ginger Liqueur

1½ oz. Orange Juice

splash Rose's Grenadine

Combine over ice.

CAPE CODDER

1¼ oz. Vox Vodka

3 oz. Cranberry Juice

dash Lime Juice

Combine in a chilled cocktail glass over ice.

CAPE FRANCE

1 oz. Cointreau

1 oz. Vox Vodka

3 oz. Cranberry juice

Lime wedge

In a tall glass, combine ingredients over ice and stir. Garnish with a wedge of lime.

CAPPUCCINO DISARONNO

Pour 1½ oz. Disaronno Amaretto into a coffee cup. Fill with fresh cappuccino.

CAPPUCCINO WITH BOMBAY SAPPHIRE GIN

Float ½ oz. Bombay Sapphire Gin on top the foamy milk of a cup of cappuccino.

CARAMEL APPLE

2 parts DeKuyper Sour Apple Pucker

1 part DeKuyper ButterShots

Chill and serve as a shot.

CAROLANS DUBLIN DOUBLE

1 part Carolans Irish Cream

1 part Disaronno Amaretto

Serve in a shot glass.

CAROLANS FIZZ

1 part Carolans Irish Cream

1 part Soda water

Fresh whipped cream

⅓ glass Crushed ice

Pour over crushed ice. Add fresh whipped cream and serve.

CAROLANS CONCERTO COFFEE

Equal parts Carolans Irish Cream and Tia Maria. Stir in coffee.

CAROLARETTO

1 part Carolans Irish Cream

1 part Disaronno Amaretto

Shake or stir on the rocks.

CASCADE MARTINI

1½ parts VOX Raspberry Vodka

1½ parts Cranberry juice

½ part Freshly squeezed lemon juice

¼ part Chambord

¼ part Vanilla syrup

12 fresh Raspberries

Shake all ingredients with ice and strain into glass.

CASSIS COCKTAIL

1 oz. Knob Creek Bourbon

½ oz. Martini & Rossi Dry Vermouth

1 tsp. DeKuyper Crème de Cassis

Shake with cracked ice. Strain into a chilled cocktail glass.

CAVALIER

1½ oz. Jose Cuervo Tequila

½ oz. Galliano

1½ oz. Orange Juice

½ oz. Cream

Shake with ice and strain into a cocktail glass.

CAZUELA

3 parts Jose Cuervo Especial

1 tsp. Grenadine

Squirt®

1 dash Salt

1 slice Lime and Lemon

1 slice Orange

1 slice Grapefruit

Put salt, lime, orange, grapefruit, lemon, and ice in a cazuela (a clay bowl commonly found in La Barca, Jalisco, Mexico). NOTE: It is important to use a cazuela that is approximately 500 ml (15 oz.). Add grenadine and Jose Cuervo Especial. Then fill with Squirt and stir.

CELTIC
BULL

1½ oz. Tullamore Dew Irish
        Whiskey

2 oz. Beef Consommé or
       Bouillon

2 oz. Tomato Juice

1-2 dashes Worcestershire
       Sauce

dash Tabasco Sauce

dash Freshly Ground
      Pepper

Shake and pour into a chilled
highball glass.

*A variation of the Bloody Bull,
which is derived from the
Bloody Mary.*

CEMENT
MIXER

¾ shot Carolans Irish
        Cream

¼ shot Lime Juice

Pour ingredients directly into
the glass. Let the drink stand
for 8 seconds.

CHAMBORD
& CHAMPAGNE

1 oz. of Chambord at the
bottom of the glass. Fill with
Champagne.

CHAMBORD & COFFEE

Add Chambord to a cup of coffee. Top with whipped cream.

CHAMBORD & COGNAC

½ Chambord

½ Hennessy Cognac

Serve in a brandy snifter.

CHAMBORD & VOX VODKA SPLASH

Martini glass half-filled with ice. ½ oz. Vox Vodka, ½ oz. Chambord. Fill with sparkling water, garnish with orange slice.

CHAMBORD ADRENALIN

½ oz. Chambord

½ oz. Vox Vodka

Shake with ice. Strain into shot glass.

CHAMBORD COLADA

1½ oz. Chambord

1½ oz. Bacardi Rum

2 oz. Pineapple juice

½ oz. Coco Lopez Real Cream of Coconut

¾ cup Ice

Blend.

CHAMBORD FROST

1½ oz. Chambord

juice of ¼ Lemon

1 cup Crushed ice

Blend or shake and pour into an ice-filled glass.

CHAMBORD ICEBERG

½ oz. Chambord

½ oz. Vox Vodka

Combine in a champagne glass packed to the top with ice.

CHAMBORD KAMIKAZI

1 oz. Vox Vodka

½ oz. Chambord

¼ oz. Cointreau

¼ oz. Lime Juice

Shake and strain into a shot glass.

CHAMBORD MARGARITA

1½ oz. Jose Cuervo Tequila

½ oz. Chambord

1 oz. Cointreau

Juice of ½ lime

Blend with an equal amount of ice until smooth.

CHAMBORD MARTINI

½ oz. Chambord

2½ oz. Vox Vodka

Pour off the ice.

CHAMBORD MOJITO

1 oz. Chambord

½ glass limes squeezed

5 mint leaves

¾ oz. sugar syrup

2 oz. Bacardi Light Rum

Muddle mint leaves, fill with rum, Chambord and ice in a tall glass. Top with club soda.

CHAMBORD PEACHY ROSE GIMLET

1 oz. Chambord

1 oz. Bombay Gin

2 oz. Sweet and sour mix

1 oz. Peachy Rose mix (homemade puree peaches and essence of rose)

Ice

Shake or stir, garnish with a lime.

CHAMBORD SIDECAR

1½ oz. Hennessy Cognac

½ oz. Cointreau

2 oz. Sweet and sour mix

2 oz. Chambord

Shake with ice, strain into sugar rimmed martini glass.

CHAMBORD SPIRIT

½ oz. Chambord

½ oz. Wild Spirit

Pour over lots of ice.

CHAMBUIE

½ oz. Drambuie

3 oz. Champagne

Pour Drambuie into Champagne flute. Top with Champagne.

CHAMPAGNE COCKTAIL

3 oz. Champagne, chilled

1 cube Sugar

dash Angostura Bitters

Stir ingredients slowly. Garnish with a Lemon Twist.

CHAMU

½ oz. Chambord

1 oz. Bacardi Rum

½ oz. Vox Vodka

3 oz. Pineapple Juice

Combine ingredients in a tall glass with ice. Fill with Pineapple Juice.

CHAPEL HILL

1¾ oz. Knob Creek Bourbon

½ oz. Cointreau

1 Tbs. Lemon Juice

Shake with ice and strain into cocktail glass. Add twist of orange peel.

CHARRO NEGRO

2 parts Jose Cuervo Especial

Coca-Cola®

Juice of ½ Lemon

Salt

Rub the rim of a chilled tall highball glass with lemon juice and dip it into the salt to coat. Put ice into the glass; add Jose Cuervo Especial and juice of half a lemon. Add some more salt if you'd like and fill the glass with Coca-Cola.

CHERI APE

1 oz. DeKuyper Cheri-Beri Pucker

½ oz. DeKuyper Blue Curacao

Add ice, fill with sweet & sour mix.

CHERI

2 oz. DeKuyper Cheri-Beri Pucker

½ oz. Bacardi Rum

7-Up

Serve in a glass, top with 7-Up.

CHERI FIZZ

1 oz. DeKuyper Cheri-Beri Pucker

½ oz. DeKuyper San Tropique

splash 7-Up

Add ice, fill with 7-Up.

CHERI PUCKER JELLO SHOTS

2 oz. DeKuyper Cheri-Beri Pucker

Ice

2 oz. Orange Juice

Pour Pucker on top. Let it filter through juice, stir.

CHERI ROYALE

DeKuyper Cheri-Beri Pucker, Vanilla Ice Cream. Blend, serve in a low ball glass.

CHERI SODA

DeKuyper Cheri-Beri Pucker, DeKuyper Thrilla Vanilla, 2 scoops of vanilla ice cream. Blend. Fill soda glass with ¾ oz. carbonated water. Garnished with whipped cream. Top with Maraschino cherry.

CHERI VANILLA POP

1 oz. DeKuyper Thrilla Vanilla

1 oz. DeKuyper Cheri-Beri Pucker

Serve as a shot or over ice.

CHERI-BERI COLADA

1 oz. DeKuyper Cheri-Beri Pucker

1 oz. Bacardi Rum

fill Piña Colada Mix

Blend ingredients. Top with ½ oz. floater of DeKuyper Cheri-Beri Pucker, garnish with a Maraschino cherry.

CHERI-BERI MARGARITA

Normal margarita recipe but substitute DeKuyper Cheri-Beri Pucker for Cointreau.

CHERI-BOMB

1 oz. DeKuyper Cheri-Beri Pucker

1 oz. DeKuyper Hot Damn!

Serve as a shot.

CHERI-COLA

1 part DeKuyper
    Cheri-Beri Pucker

Fill glass with cola; serve as a mixed drink.

CHERRY BLOSSOM

2 oz. Hennessy Cognac

¾ oz. Cointreau

½ oz. DeKuyper Cherry
    Brandy

½ oz. Lemon Juice

1 oz. Rose's Grenadine

Shake with ice and strain into glass. Garnish with Maraschino cherry.

CHERRY BOMB

½ oz. DeKuyper Cherry
    Brandy

1 oz. Bacardi Rum

½ oz. Sour Mix

Shake with ice and strain into a shot glass.

CHERRY CREAM

2 parts DeKuyper
    Cheri-Beri Pucker

1 part Bacardi Spice Rum

Fill with cream. Splash of club soda.

CHERRY ICE

1½ oz. DeKuyper
    Cheri-Beri Pucker

4 oz. Ice Cream

Blend with Ice.

CHERRY LIFESAVER

¾ oz. Disaronno Amaretto

¾ oz. Vox Vodka

1 oz. Cranberry Juice

Shake with ice; strain into cocktail glass.

CHERRY POPPIN' PINATA

2 parts DeKuyper Cheri-Beri Pucker

2 parts Jose Cuervo Tequila

Shake with ice, serve as a shot or over ice.

CHI CHI

$1\frac{1}{2}$ oz. Vox Vodka

$\frac{3}{4}$ oz. Pineapple Juice

$1\frac{1}{2}$ oz. Cream of Coconut

Blend and add a Maraschino cherry.

CHICAGO

2 oz. Hennessy Cognac

$\frac{1}{4}$ oz. Cointreau

Lemon Wedge

Superfine Sugar

Angostura bitters

Champagne

Shake with ice and strain into a wine glass. Fill with cold champagne.

CHICAGO MARTINI

$2\frac{1}{2}$ oz. Vox Vodka served in a glass rinsed with Cointreau.

CHICAGO STYLE

$\frac{3}{4}$ oz. Bacardi Light Rum

$\frac{1}{4}$ oz. Cointreau

$\frac{1}{4}$ oz. DeKuyper Anisette

$\frac{1}{4}$ oz. Lemon or Lime Juice

Blend with ice.

CHICAGO VIEW

2 oz. Bacardi O™

$\frac{1}{2}$ oz. Chambord

2 oz. Passion Fruit Juice

Shake with ice and serve over ice.

CHINA BEACH

¾ oz. Canton Delicate
        Ginger Liqueur

1 oz. Cranberry Juice

splash Vox Vodka

Shake with ice and serve over ice.

CHINESE TORTURE

1 part Canton Delicate
        Ginger Liqueur

1 part Bacardi 151 Rum

Shake with ice and strain into a shot glass.

CHOCOLATE COVERED CHERI

¾ oz. DeKuyper
        Cheri-Beri Pucker

½ oz. DeKuyper Thrilla
        Vanilla

1½ - 2 oz. Cream

Shake with ice, serve on the rocks.

CHOCOLATE MARTINI

1 oz. Vox Vodka

½ oz. Chocolate Liqueur

Shake over ice; strain into a chilled cocktail glass.

CIDER AND TEQUILA HOT TODDY

½ cup Jose Cuervo Especial

4 cups Apple Cider

1 cup Cranberry Juice

¼ cup Cointreau

       Lime Slices

In a saucepan, heat cider and cranberry juice cocktail just until hot (do not let boil) and remove from heat. Stir in Jose Cuervo Especial and Cointreau. Serve toddies in mugs, garnished with lime slices. Makes about 6 cups.

CIDER SENSATION

1 oz. DeKuyper Sour Apple Pucker

¾ oz. Apple cider

Serve over ice.

CINNAMON APPLE MARGARITA

1½ oz. Jose Cuervo Tequila

1 oz. DeKuyper Sour Apple Pucker

3 oz. Sweet & sour mix

1 oz. Orange juice

2 oz. 7-Up

DeKuyper Hot Damn!

Blend all of the ingredients together, top with ½ oz. DeKuyper Hot Damn!

CLAM VOYAGE

1 oz. Bacardi Light or Dark Rum

¼ oz. Apple Flavored Brandy

1 oz. Orange Juice

dash Orange Bitters

Blend with ice and serve in a margarita glass.

CLAMDIGGER

1¼ oz. Vox Vodka

3 oz. Mott's Clamato Juice

dash Tabasco Sauce

dash Worcestershire Sauce

Combine in mixing glass, stir well. Add ice and strain into chilled old-fashioned glass. Garnish with a lemon peel.

CLARIDGE CLASSIC

2 oz. Bombay Sapphire Gin

⅛ oz. Martini & Rossi Extra Dry Vermouth

Brine from cocktail olives

Cocktail olives garnish

Shake with ice. Strain into martini glass, add olive.

COCKTAIL NA MARA (COCKTAIL OF THE SEA)

2 oz. Tullamore Dew Irish Whiskey

2 oz. Clam Juice

4 oz. Tomato Juice

½ oz. Lemon Juice

3-4 dashes Worcestershire Sauce

dash Tabasco Sauce

pinch White Pepper

Stir all ingredients well in a mixing glass with cracked ice and pour into a chilled highball glass.

COCO COPA

Bacardi Coco, splashes of banana nectar, pineapple juice, white chocolate liqueur, and grenadine; served on ice with orange slice garnish, Maraschino cherry and flower pick.

CÓCO JUICE

¾ oz. Bacardi Rum

¾ oz. Bombay Sapphire Gin

1 oz. Pineapple juice

1 oz. Cranberry juice

Shake all ingredients with ice and pour over ice into tall glass.

COCO LOCO
(CRAZY COCONUT)

1½ oz. Jose Cuervo Tequila

3 oz. Pineapple Juice

2 oz. Coco Lopez
Cream of Coconut

Blend. Garnish with a
Pineapple Spear.

COCO MARGARITA

1¼ oz. Jose Cuervo 1800
Tequila

1 oz. Sweet & Sour Mix

1½ oz. Pineapple Juice

½ oz. Fresh Lime Juice

½ oz. Coco Lopez Cream
of Coconut

Shake or blend ingredients.
Garnish with fresh Pineapple.

COCOLOU

1 part Carolans Irish
Cream

1 part DeKuyper Crème de
Cacao

Stir well over ice.

COCOMISTICO

½ oz. Jose Cuervo Mistico

½ oz. Carolans Irish
Cream

½ oz. Chocolate Liqueur

1 oz. Half & Half

Shake ingredients and strain
into a rocks glass.

COCOMOTION

4 oz. Coco Lopez Real
Cream of Coconut

2 oz. Lime juice

1½ oz. Bacardi Dark Rum

Blend and serve. Garnish with
Maraschino cherry.

COCONUT BELLINI

2 oz.   Coco Lopez Real
Cream of Coconut

3 oz.   Champagne

2 oz.   Peach Puree

½ oz.   DeKuyper Peachtree
Schnapps

1 cup   Ice

Blend.

COCONUT PUNCH

1¼ oz.   Bacardi Light or
Añejo Rum

2 oz.   Coco Lopez Real
Cream of Coconut

½ oz.   Lemon juice

3-4 Tbs.   Vanilla ice cream

Mix all ingredients in a shaker
or blender with crushed ice
and pour into a tall glass.

COFFEE COCKTAIL

1½ oz.   Hennessy Cognac

¾ oz.   Cointreau

1 oz.   Cold black coffee

Shake with ice and pour into a
snifter.

COINTREAU GINI

1½ oz.   Cointreau

Lemon-lime soda

Pour Cointreau into a tumbler
glass with ice. Fill to the top
with lemon-lime soda. Stir.

COINTREAU CAÏPIRINHA

½ Lime

1½ oz. Cointreau

Cut ½ of lime into 5 or 6 pieces. Crush the lime in the glass. Fill to the top with crushed ice. Fill with 1½ oz. of Cointreau and stir.

COINTREAU CLIP

½ oz. Lemon or lime juice

1½ oz. Cointreau

Grapefruit juice

Strain into a tumbler glass with ice. Fill with grapefruit juice. Stir. Shake lemon (or lime) juice and Cointreau with ice.

COINTREAU COLADA

½ oz. Pineapple juice

1 oz. Cointreau

1½ oz. Bacardi Cóco

Blend pineapple juice, Cointreau and Bacardi Cóco with ice. Strain into a tumbler glass with ice. Stir. Add a drop of grenadine.

COINTREAU FIZZ

1 tsp. Sugar (or sugarcane syrup)

Juice of 1 lemon

1½ oz. Cointreau

Soda water

Shake sugar, fresh lemon juice and Cointreau with ice. Strain into a tumbler glass. Fill with soda water.

COINTREAU GRAPEFRUIT

1½ oz. Cointreau

Grapefruit juice

Pour Cointreau in a tumbler glass with ice. Fill with grapefruit juice. Stir.

COINTREAU SPARKLE

1 oz. Cointreau

Chilled sparkling white wine

Pour Cointreau into a champagne glass. Fill with chilled sparkling white wine.

COINTREAU SANTA FE MARGARITA

1½ oz. Jose Cuervo Gold Tequila

¾ oz. Cointreau

2 oz. Sweet & Sour Mix

2 oz. Cranberry Juice

Blend ingredients and serve in a margarita glass.

COINTREAU STRAWBERRY MARGARITA

1¼ oz. Jose Cuervo Gold Tequila

¾ oz. Cointreau

2 oz. Sweet & Sour Mix

3 oz. Frozen Strawberries

Blend ingredients and serve in a margarita glass.

COINTREAU TONIC

1½ oz. Cointreau

Tonic water

Pour Cointreau into a tumbler glass full of ice. Fill with tonic water. Stir.

COINTREAU MARTINI

⅛ oz. Cointreau

2 oz. Vox Vodka

Shake with ice. Serve over ice or up.

COLD IRISH

1½ oz. Tullamore Dew Irish Whiskey

½ oz. Irish Mist

2-3 drops DeKuyper Crème de Cacao

Whipped Cream

Coffee Soda

Pour the Tullamore Dew Irish Whiskey and the Irish Mist over ice. Fill with Coffee Soda and stir. Touch up the Whipped Cream with the Crème de Cacao and use it to top the drink.

COLORADO BULLDOG

1½ oz. DeKuyper Coffee Liqueur

4 oz. Cream

splash Cola

Pour first two ingredients over ice. Add a splash of Cola. Stir.

COLUMBUS COCKTAIL

1½ oz. Bacardi Rum

¾ oz. DeKuyper Apricot Brandy

Juice of ½ Lime

Mix or blend with crushed ice.

COMFORT & CREAM

½ oz. Southern Comfort

½ oz. Carolans Irish Cream

Shake.

COMFORT COLADA

1 jigger (1½ oz.) Southern Comfort, 1 oz. Coco Lopez Real Cream of Coconut, 2 oz. unsweetened pineapple juice. Shake with ½ cup crushed ice or use blender.

COMFORT MOCHA

1½ oz. Southern Comfort

1 tsp. Instant cocoa or hot chocolate

1 tsp. Instant coffee

Add boiling water. Top with whipped cream.

COMFORTING COFFEE

1½ oz. Southern Comfort

½ oz. DeKuyper Dark Creme de Cacao

Coffee

COMMANDO FIX

2 oz. Tullamore Dew Irish Whiskey

¼ oz. Cointreau

½ oz. Lime Juice

Fill a glass with ice. Add Irish Whiskey, Cointreau, and Lime Juice. Stir slowly.

COMMODORE

1 part Knob Creek Bourbon

1 part DeKuyper Crème de Cacao

1 part Sweetened Lemon Juice

1 dash Rose's Grenadine

Shake with ice and serve over ice.

CONCHITA

1¼ oz. Jose Cuervo Tequila

½ oz. Lemon Juice

6 oz. Grapefruit Juice

Combine first two ingredients in a chilled highball glass. Fill with Grapefruit Juice and stir.

CONTINENTAL

1 oz. Bacardi Light Rum

¼ oz. DeKuyper Green Crème de Menthe

¾ oz. Rose's Lime Juice

¼ tsp. Sugar (optional)

Blend with ice.

COOL MIST

2 oz. Irish Mist

Tonic Water

Combine in a tall glass with crushed ice. Add a Shamrock for a garnish.

COOPERHEAD

1¼ oz. Vox Vodka

Ginger Ale

In a tall glass filled with ice, add a squeeze of lime and garnish with lime wedge.

COPPER ILLUSION MARTINI

¼ oz. Cointreau

¼ oz. Campari

2½ oz. Bombay Sapphire Gin

Martini mixing glass filled with ice. Orange twist for garnish.

Michael Vezzoni
The Four Seasons Olympic Hotel
Seattle, WA

CORK COMFORT

1½ oz. Tullamore Dew Irish Whiskey

¾ oz. Martini & Rossi Rosso Vermouth

3-4 dashes Angostura Bitters

3-4 dashes Southern Comfort

Shake with ice. Pour into a chilled rocks glass.

CORKSCREW

¾ oz. Bacardi Light Rum

¼ oz. Brandy

¼ oz. Port Wine

½ oz. Lemon or Rose's Lime Juice

Stir. Serve over ice.

CORNET MARTINI

1½ oz. Bombay Sapphire Gin

dash Wine

Stir in cocktail glass. Strain & serve straight up or on the rocks. Add lemon twist or olives.

CORPSE REVIVER

1½ oz. Laird's Applejack

¾ oz. Hennessy Cognac

½ oz. Martini & Rossi
Rosso Vermouth

Shake and strain into a chilled cocktail glass.

COSMO KAZI

4 parts Vox Vodka

1 part Cointreau

dash Lime Juice

splash Cranberry Juice

Combine ingredients and pour over ice.

COSMOPOLITAN MARTINI

1 part Cointreau

2 parts Vox Vodka

juice of ½ Lime

splash Cranberry Juice

Shake with ice and strain.

COSSACK CHARGE

1½ oz. Vox Vodka

½ oz. Hennessey Cognac

½ oz. DeKuyper Cherry
Brandy

Mix all ingredients with cracked ice in a shaker or blender and pour into a chilled cocktail glass.

COW PUNCHER

1 oz. Bacardi Light or Dark Rum

1 oz. DeKuyper White Crème de Cacao

Milk

Pour Bacardi and Crème de Cacao into a tall glass half filled with ice. Fill with Milk.

COWBOY MARTINI

2 oz. Bombay Sapphire Gin

Sugar syrup

Fresh mint leaves

Orange bitters

Shake with ice and strain into martini glass.

CRAN-APPLE

1 oz. DeKuyper Sour Apple Pucker

$\frac{1}{2}$ oz. Vox Vodka

Cranberry juice

Serve as a shot or a drink.

CRANBERRY LARGO

$1\frac{1}{2}$ oz. DeKuyper Key Largo Tropical Schnapps

Cranberry juice

Pour Key Largo over ice into a highball glass. Add cranberry juice to fill. Garnish with lemon or lime.

CRANBERRY MARGARITA

$1\frac{1}{2}$ parts Jose Cuervo Especial

3 parts Jose Cuervo Margarita Mix

dash Cranberry Juice

Handful of Frozen Cranberries

Blend all ingredients in a blender with one scoop of crushed ice. Pour entire contents into a margarita glass. NOTE: The cranberries should fleck throughout the drink.

CRANJACK

1½ oz. Laird's Applejack

4 oz. Club Soda

splash Cranberry Juice

Pour Laird's Applejack over ice in a tall glass. Add club soda with a splash of cranberry juice. Garnish with lime if desired.

CRAN-RUM TWISTER

2 oz. Bacardi Light Rum

3 oz. Cranberry Juice

Lemon-Lime Soda

Combine the first two ingredients in a tall glass with ice. Fill with Lemon-Lime Soda and garnish with a Lemon Slice.

CRANTINI

2 oz. Bacardi Limón

touch Martini & Rossi Extra Dry Vermouth

splash Cranberry Juice

Shake and serve straight up. Garnish with Cranberries and a Lemon Twist.

CRAZY PUCKER

1 part DeKuyper Sour Apple Pucker

1 part DeKuyper Cheri-Beri Pucker

1 part DeKuyper Grape Pucker

1 part Vox Vodka

squeeze Lime

Top with cola, in a tall glass.

CREAM WHISKEY

1 part Carolans Irish
Cream

2 parts Rye Whiskey

Stir well over ice.

CREAMED IRISH COFFEE

2 oz. Carolans Irish
Cream

Hot coffee

Add sugar to taste.

CREAMED SHERRY

2 parts Carolans Irish
Cream

1 part Duff Gordon Cream
Sherry

Stir well over ice.

CREAMSICKLE

¾ oz. Disaronno Amaretto

¾ oz. Cointreau

½ oz. Orange Juice

1½ oz. Cream

Blend with ice. Serve in wine
glass.

CREAMSICLE

½ oz. Cointreau

½ oz. Liquore Galliano

1 oz. Cream

Orange Juice

Shake with ice and strain.

CREAMY IRISH COFFEE

1½ oz. Carolans Irish
Cream

Fill with hot coffee. Top with
whipped cream.

CREOLE

1¾ oz. Bacardi Light Rum

2 splashes Lemon

3½ oz. Beef Bouillon

dash Pepper

dash Salt

dash Tabasco Sauce

dash Worcestershire
Sauce

Combine over ice.

CREOLE LADY

1½ oz. Knob Creek
Bourbon

1 oz. Madeira

1 tsp. Grenadine

Stir with ice and strain into cocktail glass. Serve with one green and one maraschino red cherry.

CREST OF THE WAVE

1¼ oz. Bombay Sapphire
Gin

1½ oz. Grapefruit juice

1½ oz. Cranberry juice

Shake with ice. Serve in a tall glass.

CRICKET

¾ oz. Bacardi Light Rum

¼ oz. DeKuyper White
Crème de Cacao

¼ oz. DeKuyper Green
Crème de Menthe

1 oz. Cream

Blend.

CRISP SUNSET

2 oz. Bombay Sapphire
Gin

1 Tbs. Pineapple Juice

½ oz. Cointreau

Mix ingredients with cracked ice in shaker; strain into martini glass.

CUBA LIBRE

1¾ oz. Bacardi Rum

Cola

Juice of ¼ Lime

Add Bacardi to a glass filled with ice. Fill with Cola. Add Lime Juice and stir.

CUCARACHA

½ part Jose Cuervo Especial

½ part DeKuyper Coffee Liqueur

Pour Jose Cuervo Especial and DeKuyper Coffee Liqueur into a shot glass.

CUERVO AND TONIC

2 parts Jose Cuervo Especial

Chilled Tonic Water

¼ Lime

2 Thin Lime Slice

Coarse Salt

Rub the rim of a tall highball glass with the ¼ lime and dip it into a bowl of coarse salt to coat it lightly. Fill glass with ice and squeeze remaining lime juice into it. Add Jose Cuervo Especial and stir. Fill with tonic water. Garnish with lime slices.

CUERVO ALEXANDER

1 oz. Jose Cuervo Gold Tequila

1 oz. DeKuyper Coffee Liqueur

1 oz. DeKuyper Cherry Brandy

2 scoops Vanilla Ice Cream

Blend until smooth.

CUERVO COOLER

2 parts Jose Cuervo Especial

2 parts Cuarenta y Tres
(Licor 43)

Seltzer or Club Soda

Fill a rocks glass three-fourths full of ice cubes, stir together tequila and Licor 43. Top off with seltzer or club soda. Stir well.

CUERVO DREAM

2 parts Jose Cuervo Especial

1½ parts Martini & Rossi Dry Vermouth

1½ parts Martini & Rossi Rosso Vermouth

Maraschino Cherry

Pour Jose Cuervo Especial and the Vermouths into a cocktail shaker with ice cubes. Shake well. Strain into a chilled martini glass. Garnish with marashino cherry.

CUERVO FRESCA

2 parts Jose Cuervo Especial

Lemonade

Grapefruit

Lime

Slice of Melon

Few Raspberries

Shake all ingredients (except lemonade) in a cocktail shaker and strain over fresh ice into a rocks glass. Top with lemonade. This works with almost any fruit, herb or vegetable. Try honey and basil or port and blackberries.

CUERVO MOJITO

2 parts	Jose Cuervo Especial
8	Fresh Mint Leaves
1½ Tbs.	Superfine Granulated Sugar
1 Tbs.	Lime Juice
⅓ cup	Chilled Sparkling Water

Using the back of a spoon, crush mint with sugar and lime juice in a rocks glass. Fill half of the glass with ice and add Jose Cuervo Especial. Top off drink with sparkling water and stir well.

CUERVO SHAKE

3 parts	Jose Cuervo Especial
1 tsp.	Honey
1	Egg White
6 dashes	Orange Bitters
	Juice of one Lime
	Sparkling Water
	Lime Slice

Shake all ingredients (except sparkling water and lime slice) in a cocktail shaker. Pour into a chilled rocks glass filled with ice cubes. Finish it off with sparkling water and garnish with a lime slice.

CUERVO SIDE-OUT

1½ oz.	Jose Cuervo Gold Tequila
1 oz.	Cointreau
2 oz.	Cranberry Juice
1½ oz.	Lime Juice

Blend.

CUERVO STINGER

2 parts Jose Cuervo Especial

2 parts DeKuyper Crème de Menthe (White)

Pour Jose Cuervo Especial and Crème de Menthe into a mixing glass with ice cubes. Shake well. Strain into a chilled martini glass.

CUERVO SUNRISE

1½ oz. Jose Cuervo Gold Tequila

3 oz. Cranberry Juice

½ oz. Lime Juice

½ oz. Rose's Grenadine

Shake and serve over ice. Garnish with a Lime.

CUERVO SUNRISE II

2 parts Jose Cuervo Especial

2 parts Rose's Grenadine

Orange Juice

Pineapple Wedge

Pour Jose Cuervo Especial into a chilled tall highball glass over ice. Fill the glass with orange juice leaving a little room on top and stir. Slowly pour in the grenadine. Garnish with pineapple wedge.

CUERVO TEQUINI

3 parts Jose Cuervo Especial

½ part Martini & Rossi Dry Vermouth

dash Angostura Bitters

Garnish with lemon twist.

CUERVO TROPICAL

1½ oz. Jose Cuervo Gold Tequila

3 oz. Orange Juice

1 tsp. Lemon Juice

½ oz. Rose's Grenadine

Mix in highball glass filled with cracked ice.

Garnish with half an Orange Slice and a Maraschino Cherry.

CUERVOPOLITAN

1¼ oz. Cuervo Añejo Tequila

¼ oz. Cointreau

½ oz. Cranberry juice

juice of ½ lime

Pour all ingredients into a shaker filled with ice and stir vigorously. Strain into a chilled martini glass.

DEEP RAZZY

6 oz. Bacardi Razz

1 oz. Cointreau

1 oz. Chambord

1 oz. Sweet & sour

½ oz. Fresh lime juice

Shake and strain all ingredients into a chilled 10 oz. martini glass. Garnish with three skewered raspberries and a fresh sprig of mint.

DEEP SEA MARTINI

1½ oz. Bombay Sapphire Gin

1 oz. Martini & Rossi Dry Vermouth

1 dash Orange Bitters

¼ oz. Pernod

Stir with ice, strain into martini glass. Garnish with lemon peel.

DEPTH CHARGE MARTINI

1¼ oz.   Bombay Sapphire Gin

1¼ oz.   Lillet

¼ oz.   Pernod

Orange peel

Stir with ice, strain into martini glass.

DEWAR'S SIDECAR

1½ oz.   Dewar's White Label Blended Scotch Whisky

½ oz.   Cointreau

1 oz.   Sour & Sour mix

Optional garnish: Maraschino cherry or orange peel.

DEWAR'S & SEVEN NATIONS

A light, refreshing drink that sings of Celtic passion.

2 oz.   Dewar's White Label

fill   7-Up or Sprite

In highball glass over ice.

DEWAR'S 12 AND CRANBERRY*

2 oz.   Dewar's 12 Year Old

Serve neat.

*Note: Cranberries should never be mixed with Dewar's 12, as they would mar the robust, full flavor. Please use cranberries responsibly and bake in muffins or fruitcake, where they belong.

DEWAR'S 12 AND SODA

Dewar's 12 uses Scotland's finest 12-year-old whiskies to create its harmonious blend.

Share this harmony with 2 oz. of Dewar's 12 and a splash of soda.

122

DEWAR'S 12 AND WATER

2 oz. Dewar's 12

Serve in an old-fashioned glass over ice with a splash of water.

DEWAR'S 12 ESKIMO KISS*

2 oz. Dewar's 12 Year Old

Serve over ice with a splash of soda.

*Given the typical response when a host receives the thoughtful and elegant gift of Dewar's 12 Year Old, mistletoe may not be required. *Dewar's 12 Year Old takes the extra step of "marrying" its whiskies in oak casks, allowing them to mix and mingle to create a layered scotch of unsurpassed smoothness.

DEWAR'S 12 MANHATTAN

Shake things up with a new twist on an old favorite.

1½ oz. Dewar's 12

½ oz. Martini & Rossi Rosso Vermouth

1 dash Aromatic Bitters

Chill all ingredients in a cocktail shaker; strain and serve straight up in a chilled martini glass. Optional: garnish with cherry or twist of lemon.

DEWAR'S 12 NEAT

2 oz. Dewar's 12

The only deluxe 12-year-old blended scotch whisky to win Double Gold two years in a row, at the San Francisco World Spirits Competition. Try it neat to enjoy the clean and pleasant finish that sets Dewar's 12 apart.

Serve neat.

DEWAR'S 12 PEPPERMINT TWIST*

2 oz. Dewar's 12 Year Old

Serve over ice with a splash of water.

*Distract fidgety family members with candy canes to ensure serenity while you enjoy your Dewar's 12.

DEWAR'S 12 ROCKS

At 86 Proof, Dewar's 12 stands up to ice better than most deluxes. Pour 2 oz. of Dewar's 12 in a glass, fill it up with ice and enjoy its smooth, full flavor.

DEWAR'S 12 RUSTY NAIL

A slightly sweet and satisfying experience.

1½ oz. Dewar's 12

½ oz. Drambuie

Serve in an old-fashioned glass over ice.

DEWAR'S DRY ROB ROY

3 parts Dewar's White Label

1 part Martini & Rossi Dry Vermouth

Stir and serve on the rocks or up. Add twist of lemon.

DEWAR'S HIGHBALL

A mouthwatering spin on America's favorite scotch whisky.

2 oz. Dewar's White Label

fill Ginger Ale

Serve in a highball glass over ice and garnish with orange or lime.

DEWAR'S HIGHLANDER

A tantalizing libation that stands tall.

2 oz. Dewar's White Label

juice of ½ Lime

Serve in a highball glass over ice.

DEWAR'S MANHATTAN

Shake things up with a new twist on an old favorite.

1½ oz. Dewar's White Label

½ oz. Martini & Rossi
Rosso Vermouth

1 dash Aromatic Bitters

Chill all ingredients in a cocktail shaker; strain and serve straight up in a chilled martini glass. Optional: garnish with cherry or twist of lemon.

DEWAR'S OLD-FASHIONED

2½ oz. Dewar's White Label

¼ tsp. Sugar

2 dashes Angostura Bitters

Muddle cherry and orange slice in bottom of old-fashioned glass. Add ingredients and stir well. Top with club soda or water.

DEWAR'S PERFECT ROB ROY

3 parts Dewar's White Label

1 part Martini & Rossi
Rosso Vermouth

1 part Martini & Rossi Dry
Vermouth

Stir and serve on the rocks or up. Add cherry or a twist.

DEWAR'S ROB ROY

3 parts Dewar's White Label

2 parts Martini & Rossi
Rosso Vermouth

Stir and serve on the rocks or up. Add cherry or a twist.

DEWAR'S ROCKS

The classic way for an established scotch consumer to enjoy the sophisticated finish of the Dewar's White Label Blend. 2 oz. Dewar's White Label. Serve in an old-fashioned glass over ice.

DEWAR'S RUSTY NAIL

A slightly sweet and satisfying experience.

1½ oz. Dewar's White Label

½ oz. Drambuie

Serve in an old-fashioned glass over ice.

DEWAR'S SIDECAR

1½ oz. Dewar's White Label

¾ oz. Cointreau

¾ oz. Sweetened Lemon
        Juice

Shake and serve in sugar-rimmed cocktail glass.

DEWAR'S SLING

Dewar's White Label, sugar syrup, lemon juice and water. Serve over ice in a rocks glass.

DEWAR'S SOUR

The perfect balance of sour and sweet, a tempting varia-tion on the classic recipe.

2 oz. Dewar's White Label

1½ oz. Sweet & Sour Mix

Serve in a highball or rocks glass over ice.

DEWAR'S SPLASH

Adding a splash of water "opens up" the whisky so scotch drinkers can appreciate the perfect balance of smoky and sweet notes.

2 oz. Dewar's White Label

Serve in an old-fashioned glass with a splash of water.

DEWAR'S TWIST

1¼ oz. Dewar's White Label

splash Water

Serve in rocks glass with ice. Garnish with a lemon twist.

DEWEY MARTINI

1½ oz. Vox Vodka

dash Martini & Rossi
       Extra Dry Vermouth

dash Orange Bitters

Shake and strain into a cock-tail glass or serve over ice.

DIABLO

2 parts Jose Cuervo Especial

dash Chambord

Ginger Beer

Lime Slice

Pour Jose Cuervo Especial in a tall highball glass full of ice, leaving a little room on top. Add a dash of Chambord. Top off the drink with Ginger Beer. Garnish with lime.

DIAMONDS ARE FOREVER

2½ oz. Bombay Sapphire Gin

splash Dewar's White Label

Pour Bombay Sapphire Gin and Dewar's over ice and stir. Strain into a well-chilled martini glass. Garnish with olives.

DIMON SHOOTER

½ oz. Disaronno Amaretto

½ oz. Bacardi Limón™

Pour into a shot glass. Top off with lemon-lime soda.

DINGLE DRAM

1½ oz. Tullamore Dew Irish Whiskey

½ oz. Irish Mist

Coffee Soda

dash DeKuyper Crème de Cacao

Whipped Cream

Pour Tullamore Dew Irish Whiskey and Irish Mist into a chilled highball glass along with several ice cubes. Fill with Coffee Soda. Stir gently. Add a float of Crème de Cacao. Top with dollop of Whipped Cream.

DIRTY COOKIE

⅔ shot Carolans Irish
Cream

⅓ shot DeKuyper Green
Crème de Menthe

Shake with ice and strain into
a shot glass.

DIRTY DRIFT

1 oz. Drambuie

1 oz. DeKuyper Anisette

Serve as a shot or over ice.

DIRTY HARRY

1 oz. Cointreau

1 oz. Tia Maria

Shake with ice and strain.

DIRTY JOB

1 oz. Vox Vodka

1 oz. Cointreau

Tonic water

Pour Vox Vodka and Cointreau
into a tumbler glass full of ice.
Fill with tonic water. Stir.

DIRTY NELLY

1 oz. Carolans Irish
Cream

1 oz. Tullamore Dew
Irish Whiskey

Shake.

DISARITA MARGARITA

1 oz. Jose Cuervo 1800
Tequila

½ oz. Disaronno Amaretto

3 oz. Margarita Mix

½ cup Crushed ice

Blend.

DISARITA MARGARITA II

1 oz. Jose Cuervo 1800 Tequila

½ oz. Disaronno Amaretto

½ oz. Cointreau

3 oz. Margarita Mix

½ cup Crushed Ice

Blend. Garnish with Lime.

DISARONNO ALEXANDER

1 oz. Disaronno Amaretto

1 oz. DeKuyper Créme de Cacao

1 oz. Cream

Shake all ingredients with ice, strain into a cocktail glass, and serve.

DISARONNO AND CREAM

2 oz. Disaronno Amaretto

1 oz. Cream or Milk

Pour Disaronno and cream over ice. Stir and serve in old-fashioned glass.

DISARONNO BOCCE BALL

2 oz. Disaronno Amaretto

6 oz. Chilled Orange Juice

splash Soda

Lime slice, optional

Pour Disaronno and orange juice in a glass over ice. Add a splash of soda. Stir and garnish with a lime slice.

DISARONNO CAPPUCINO

1½ oz. Disaronno
        Amaretto

6 oz. Cappucino

Pour Disaronno into hot cappucino and serve.

DISARONNO CHERRY BOMB

2 oz. Disaronno Amaretto

4 oz. Coke or Diet Coke

Serve in rocks glass over ice. Garnish with a Maraschino cherry.

DISARONNO COSMOPOLITAN

1 oz. Disaronno Amaretto

1 oz. Bacardi Limón™

splash Cranberry Juice

Stir with ice and strain into a martini glass.

DISARONNO HOT CHOCOLATE

2 oz. Disaronno Amaretto

6 oz. Hot Chocolate

In a mug, pour Disaronno liqueur into hot chocolate. Top with whipped cream.

DISARONNO ITALIAN TICKLER

2 oz. Disaronno Amaretto

5 oz. Club soda

DISARONNO MARGARITA

1 oz. Disaronno Amaretto

3 oz. Margarita Mix

1 oz. Jose Cuervo Tequila

Shake well with ice and strain into a salt rimmed glass: garnish with lime slice.

DISARONNO MIMOSA

½ cup Disaronno Amaretto

3 cups Orange Juice

750-ml. Bottle chilled
Martini & Rossi
Asti sparkling wine

In a pitcher, stir together orange juice and Disaronno. Fill each of 6 champagne flutes halfway with juice mixture and top off with sparkling wine. Makes about 12 drinks.

DISARONNO PUNCH

1½ oz. Disaronno Amaretto

1 oz. Bacardi Limón™

3 oz. Cranberry Juice

Serve over ice.

DISARONNO ROYALE

1 oz. Disaronno Amaretto

Champagne

Pour Disaronno into a chilled champagne flute. Top off with champagne.

DISARONNO SOUR

2 oz. Disaronno Amaretto

4 oz. Sweet & Sour Mix

Combine ingredients with cracked ice in a cocktail shaker. Shake well and strain into chilled, sugar-rimmed glass over ice cubes.

DISARONNO SUNRISE

1½ oz. Disaronno Amaretto

1 oz. Bacardi Rum

3 oz. Orange Juice

Serve over ice in a tall glass.

DISARONNO TICKLER

2 oz. Disaronno Amaretto

5 oz. Club Soda

Mix with ice. Serve in tall glass.

DISARONNO TOASTED ALMOND

1½ oz. Disaronno Amaretto

1 oz. Cream

1 oz. DeKuyper Coffee Liqueur

Pour Disaronno and DeKuyper Coffee Liqueur into an old-fashioned glass over ice. Float cream or milk on top by pouring it in gently over the back of a teaspoon.

DISARTINI

1 oz. Disaronno Amaretto

1 oz. Bombay Sapphire Gin

Stir (do not shake) with ice and strain into chilled martini glass. Garnish with a twist of orange rind.

DISCO

1½ oz. Mango infused Vox Vodka

½ oz. Chambord

2 oz. Cranberry juice

Shake & Pour over ice and garnish with a chocolate disc.

DIXIE DEW

1½ oz. Knob Creek
         Bourbon

½ oz.   DeKuyper White
         Crème de Menthe

½ tsp. Cointreau

In a mixing glass half-filled-
with ice cubes, combine all
of the ingredients. Stir well.
Strain into a cocktail glass.

DIXIE JULEP

1 tsp. Powdered Sugar

2 oz.   Knob Creek
         Bourbon

Put sugar and Bourbon into
collins glass. Fill with crushed
ice and stir gently. Decorate
with sprigs of mint.

DIXIE STINGER

3 oz.   Knob Creek
         Bourbon

½ oz.   DeKuyper White
         Crème de Menthe

½ tsp. Southern
         Comfort

In a shaker half-filled with ice
cubes, combine all of the
ingredients. Shake well. Strain
into a cocktail glass.

DIXIE WHISKEY COCKTAIL

2 oz.   Knob Creek
         Bourbon

½ tsp. DeKuyper White
         Creme de Menthe

¼ tsp. Cointreau

½ tsp. Powdered Sugar

1 dash Bitters

Shake with ice and strain into
cocktail glass.

DIZZY LIZZY

1½ oz. Knob Creek Bourbon

1½ oz. Sherry

dash Lemon Juice

Club Soda

Combine first three ingredients in a tall glass with ice. Fill with Club Soda.

DOUBLE GOLD

½ oz. Jose Cuervo Gold Tequila

½ oz. Goldschlager

Shake with ice and strain into a shot glass.

DRAMBUIE AFTER

After dining pour Drambuie into cordial glass and serve neat.

DRAMBUIE CIDER

Add 2 oz. Drambuie to hot apple cider. Add a stick of cinnamon.

DRAMBUIE COFFEE

Freshly brewed coffee lightly sweetened with the delicious flavor of Drambuie. Serve in a warm glass and top with fresh cream. Equally pleasing when served with hot tea instead of coffee. Satisfying and distinctly different.

DRAMBUIE MIST

Pour Drambuie over crushed ice and add a lemon twist.

DRAMBUIE ON ICE

A generous measure of Drambuie poured over ice. An after dinner delight.

DREAM COCKTAIL

2 oz. Hennessy Cognac

½ oz. Cointreau

1 tsp. DeKuyper Anisette

Shake with ice and strain into a cocktail glass.

DUBLIN COFFEE

1 oz. DeKuyper Coffee Liqueur

½ oz. Irish Mist

Hot coffee

Whipped cream

Serve in a coffee mug.

DUBLIN HANDSHAKE

½ oz. Carolans Irish Cream

½ oz. Tullamore Dew Irish Whiskey

¾ oz. Bombay Sapphire Gin

Shake with crushed ice. Strain into a cocktail glass.

DUBONNET COCKTAIL

1½ oz. Dubonnet

½ oz. Bombay Sapphire Gin

dash Angostura Bitters

Combine over ice.

DUCK PIN

1 oz. Chambord

1 oz. Southern Comfort

½ oz. Pineapple Juice

Shake with ice and strain into a shot glass.

DUNDEE

2 tsp. Drambuie

1½ oz. Bombay Dry Gin

2 Tbs. Dewar's Scotch

1 tsp. Lemon Juice

Fill mixing glass with ice, add Bombay, Dewar's, Drambuie and lemon juice. Shake, strain into a rocks glass and add ice. Garnish with a maraschino cherry and a lemon twist.

EAST INDIA

1½ oz. Hennessy Cognac

½ oz. Cointreau

½ oz. Pineapple juice

dash Angostura bitters

Shake and strain into a martini or wine glass.

ELECTRIC PEACH

1 oz. Vox Vodka

¼ oz. DeKuyper Peachtree
Schnapps

½ oz. Cranberry Juice
Cocktail

¼ oz. Orange Juice

Blend. Garnish with a Lemon
Slice.

ELECTRIC SCREWDRIVER

1 part Jose Cuervo Especial

1 part VOX Vodka

4 parts Orange Juice

Lemon Slice

Mix Jose Cuervo Especial,
Vodka and orange juice in a
chilled tall highball glass over
ice. Garnish with lemon slice.

ELECTRIC TICKLER

¼ oz. Drambuie

1½ oz. Bombay Dry Gin

¼ oz. Martini & Rossi
Rosso Vermouth

Orange Juice

Club Soda

In a collins glass, shake with
ice, strain over ice. Fill with
soda. Lemon garnish.

ELEGANT MARTINI BOMBAY SAPPHIRE GIN

1¾ oz. Bombay Sapphire
Gin

½ oz. Martini & Rossi
Dry Vermouth

¼ oz. Cointreau

dash Cointreau (on top)

Stir the first three ingredients
with ice. Strain or serve on
ice. Float Cointreau on top.

ELEGANT MARTINI VOX VODKA

1½ oz. Vox Vodka

dash Martini & Rossi Extra Dry Vermouth

¼ oz. Cointreau

dash Cointreau (on top)

Stir the first three ingredients with ice. Serve on ice or straight up. Cointreau on top.

ELIXIR OF LOVE

1½ oz. Disaronno Amaretto

½ oz. DeKuyper Crème de Cacao

½ oz. Bacardi Light Rum

2 oz. Cream

Serve over crushed ice.

EMERALD ISLE

¾ shot Tullamore Dew

¾ shot DeKuyper Green Creme de Menthe

2 scoops Vanilla ice cream

Soda water

Blend first 3 ingredients then add soda water. Stir after adding soda water.

ERIE TOUR

⅓ Irish Mist

⅓ Carolans Irish Cream

⅓ Tullamore Dew Irish Whiskey

Serve over ice.

ERIN GO BURRR

3 oz. Carolans Irish Cream

Serve chilled Carolans Irish Cream straight up in a chilled cocktail glass.

EVERYTHING

1 oz. Bombay Sapphire Gin

½ oz. Martini & Rossi Extra Dry Vermouth

½ oz. Martini & Rossi Rosso Vermouth

dash DeKuyper White Creme de Menthe

2 dashes Bitters

Stir on the rocks.

EYES R SMILIN'

1 oz. Carolans Irish Cream

1 oz. Vox Vodka

½ oz. Bombay Sapphire Gin

½ oz. Cointreau

Build over ice. Stir and serve.

FALLEN ANGEL

½ oz. Bombay Sapphire Gin

½ oz. DeKuyper Apricot Flavored Brandy

¼ oz. Brandy

Shake. Serve up.

FAT CAT

1 oz. Hennessy Cognac

¾ oz. Galliano

¼ oz. DeKuyper White Crème de Cacao

1 cup Vanilla ice cream

Blend until smooth. Pour into a wine goblet.

FEMME FATALE

Combine in a snifter:

2 oz. Hennessy VS

2 oz. Cranberry juice

Fill with Moet & Chandon Nectar Imperial add rocks.

FOG CUTTER

½ oz. Bombay Sapphire Gin

1½ oz. Bacardi Light Rum

½ oz. Brandy

1 oz. Orange Juice

3 Tbs. Lemon Juice

Shake all ingredients and strain into a collins glass with ice.

FOGGY DAY MARTINI

1½ oz. Bombay Sapphire Gin

¼ oz. Pernod

twist Lemon Peel

Shake and pour over ice or serve straight up. Garnish with a Lemon Twist.

FOOLS GOLD

1 part Vox Vodka

1 part Galliano

Shake with ice and strain into a shot glass.

FORBIDDEN FRUIT

½ oz. DeKuyper Sour Apple Pucker

½ oz. DeKuyper Peachtree Schnapps

½ oz. Knob Creek Bourbon

1½ oz. Sweet & sour mix

Shake with ice and serve over ice.

FOURTH DEGREE MARTINI

¾ oz. Bombay Sapphire Gin

¾ oz. Martini & Rossi Dry Vermouth

¾ oz. Martini & Rossi Rosso Vermouth

¼ oz. Pernod

Garnish with a Lemon Peel Twist. Stir gently with ice; serve straight up or over ice.

FOURTH OF JULY

⅓ shot Rose's Grenadine

⅓ shot Vox Vodka

⅓ shot DeKuyper Blue Curacao

Layer this drink in the order listed.

FREDDIE FUDPUCKER

1 oz. Jose Cuervo Tequila

4 oz. Orange Juice

½ oz. Galliano

½ oz. DeKuyper Coffee Liqueur

Shake and serve over ice.

FRENCH CREAM

1½ oz. Carolans Irish Cream

½ oz. Chambord

2 oz. Half & half

4 oz. Ice cubes

Blend.

FRENCH COLADA

1½ oz. Bacardi Light Rum

¾ oz. Hennessy Cognac

1 scoop Crushed Ice

¾ oz. Sweet Cream

¾ oz. Coco Lopez Cream of Coconut

1½ oz. Pineapple Juice

splash DeKuyper Créme de Cassis

Blend.

FRENCH KISS

2 parts Vox Vodka

1½ parts Chambord

¾ part DeKuyper White Creme de Cacao

¾ part Cream

Shake ingredients with ice and strain into glass.

FRENCH MARTINI

½ oz. Chambord

1½ oz. Vox Vodka

2 oz. Pineapple juice

Shake and pour over ice.

FRENCH SUMMER

¼ oz. Chambord

3 oz. Sparkling water

Slice lemon and orange

Pour the Chambord into a wine glass filled with ice. Add the sparkling water and the juice of a slice of lemon and orange. Stir.

FRENCH "75"

1½ oz. Bombay Sapphire Gin

2 tsp. Superfine Sugar

1½ oz. Lemon Juice

4 oz. Champagne, chilled

1 Maraschino Cherry

Shake well, except Champagne. Pour into a collins glass. Top with Champagne. Stir well and garnish with Maraschino cherry.

FRU-FRU

¾ oz. DeKuyper Creme de Banana Liqueur

1 oz. DeKuyper Peachtree Schnapps

dash Rose's Lime Juice

1 oz. Pineapple Juice

Shake with ice and strain into a shot glass.

FRUIT BLAST MARTINI COCKTAIL

1 oz. Bacardi O™

1 oz. Bacardi Tropico

1½ oz. Pineapple Juice

1 oz. Cranberry Juice

Shake with ice; strain into martini glass and garnish with strawberry.

FRUIT COCKTAIL

½ oz. each of DeKuyper Cheri-Beri and Grape Pucker. Serve as a shot or on the rocks.

FRUIT SALAD

Equal parts (½ oz. each), DeKuyper Cheri-Beri Pucker, Grape Pucker and DeKuyper Peachtree Schnapps. Splash of orange juice. Combine, serve as shot or over ice.

FRUIT SALAD II

Equal parts:

> DeKuyper Sour Apple Pucker
>
> DeKuyper Cheri-Beri Pucker
>
> DeKuyper Grape Pucker

splash Orange juice

Combine, serve as shot or over ice.

FRUIT SALAD SLAMMER

> DeKuyper Sour Apple Pucker
>
> DeKuyper Grape Pucker
>
> DeKuyper Cheri-Beri Pucker

Mix equal parts, chill and serve in a shot glass.

FRUITY IRISHMAN

2 parts Carolans Irish Cream

1 part DeKuyper Melon Liqueur

Stir.

FUDGESICLE

1 oz. Vox Vodka

¼ oz. DeKuyper Crème de Cacao

¼ oz. Chocolate Syrup

Shake and serve over ice.

FUN AT THE BEACH

1 oz. DeKuyper Peachtree Schnapps

1 oz. DeKuyper Sour Apple Pucker

3 oz. Cranberry juice

3 oz. Pineapple juice

Serve over ice in a tall glass.

FUZZ BALL

1 oz. DeKuyper Watermelon Pucker

1 oz. DeKuyper Peachtree Schnapps

Serve in shot glass.

FUZZY NAVEL

1¼ oz. DeKuyper Peachtree Schnapps

3 oz. Orange Juice

Pour Schnapps over ice in a rocks glass. Fill with Orange Juice and stir well.

FUZZY RITA

½ oz. Cointreau

1½ oz. Jose Cuervo Tequila

½ oz. DeKuyper Peachtree Schnapps

1½ oz. Lime Juice

Combine over ice in a tall glass.

GASSER

1 oz. Drambuie

1½ oz. Dewar's Scotch

1 Tbs. Martini & Rossi
Rosso Vermouth

2 dashes Orange Bitters

In an old-fashioned glass,
shake with ice, strain over ice.
Add orange twist.

GENTLEMAN'S COCKTAIL

1½ oz. Knob Creek
Bourbon

½ oz. Hennessy Cognac

½ oz. DeKuyper White
Creme de Menthe

Club Soda

Pour Bourbon, Hennessy, and
Creme de Menthe over ice
into highball glass. Add club
soda and garnish with a
lemon wheel.

GIBSON

2 oz. Bombay Dry Gin

dash Martini & Rossi
Extra Dry Vermouth

Cocktail Onion

Stir with ice. Add the Cocktail
Onion. Serve straight up or
on ice.

GIMLET

1¼ oz. Vox Vodka

½ oz. Fresh Lime Juice

Mix Vox Vodka and Lime
Juice in a glass with ice. Strain
and serve in a cocktail glass.
Garnish with a Lime Twist.

GIMLET II

2 oz. Bombay Sapphire
Gin

½ oz. Martini & Rossi
Extra Dry Vermouth

½ oz. Rose's Lime Juice

1 Lime Slice

Serve over ice.

GLOWLIGHT

½ oz. Drambuie

1½ oz. Bombay Dry Gin

½ oz. Jose Cuervo Tequila

1 tsp. Grenadine

½ tsp. Bacardi Light Rum
Club Soda

2 Maraschino
Cherries

In a collins glass, pour over
ice, fill with soda. Add grenadine and maraschino cherries.
Float Bacardi.

GODCHILD

1 oz. Disaronno Amaretto

1 oz. Vox Vodka

1 oz. Cream or Half &
Half

Shake with ice. Strain into a
chilled martini glass.

GODFATHER

1 oz. Disaronno Amaretto

1 oz. Dewar's White Label

Pour over ice in a rocks glass.

GODMOTHER

1 oz. Disaronno Amaretto

1 oz. Vox Vodka

Pour over ice in a rocks glass.

GOLD DIGGER MARTINI

½ oz. Cointreau

1 oz. Vox Vodka

½ oz. Pineapple Juice

Stir with ice; serve straight up or over ice.

GOLDEN BOY

1½ oz. Knob Creek Bourbon

½ oz. Bacardi Rum

2 oz. Orange Juice

1 tsp. Lemon Juice

1 tsp. Sugar Syrup

1 scoop Crushed Ice

dash Rose's Grenadine

Mix all ingredients, except the Rose's Grenadine, in a shaker. Strain mixture into a chilled glass. Top with a dash of Rose's Grenadine.

GOLDEN CADILLAC

¼ oz. Galliano

1 oz. DeKuyper White Crème de Cacao

1 oz. Cream

Mix in a blender with a little ice. Strain into a champagne glass. A scoop of Vanilla Ice Cream may be substituted for Cream.

GOLDEN DAY

¾ oz. Vox Vodka

½ oz. Liquore Galliano

Serve in a rocks glass over ice.

GOLDEN GIRL MARTINI

1¾ oz.   Bombay Sapphire Gin

¾ oz.   Dry Sherry

1 dash   Angostura Bitters

Stir and strain into a martini glass.

GOLDEN PEACH

¾ oz.   DeKuyper Peachtree Schnapps

1 oz.   Bombay Sapphire Gin

5 oz.   Orange Juice

In a tall glass with ice, fill with orange juice, stir well.

GOLDEN DREAM

½ oz.   Cointreau

1 oz.   Liquore Galliano

½ oz.   Orange Juice

½ oz.   Cream

Shake with cracked ice. Strain into a cocktail glass. You can also serve this over ice in a highball glass.

GOOD AND PLENTY

1 oz.   DeKuyper Anisette

1 oz.   DeKuyper Blackberry Brandy

Shake with ice and strain into a shot glass.

GOTHAM BAR & GRILL AVIATION

3½ oz. Bombay Sapphire Gin

1½ oz. Maraschino Liqueur

juice of ½ Lemon

Mix all ingredients with cracked ice in shaker; strain into martini glass. Garnish with cherry.

The Gotham Bar & Grill
NY, NY

GRAND CENTRAL MARTINI

3 oz. Bombay Sapphire Gin

3 squirts Tabasco

sm. squirt Lemon Juice

1 Blue Point Oyster, shucked

Mix all ingredients with cracked ice in shaker; strain into martini glass. Garnish with an oyster.

The Grand Central Oyster Bar
Grand Central Station
NY, NY

GRAND MARGARITA

1 oz. Jose Cuervo Tequila

¾ oz. Cointreau

Fresh lime juice

Sugar

Fill shaker with ice. Add Cuervo and the Cointreau. Fill with lime juice and add sugar to taste. Shake. Pour over ice or strain. Garnish with a lime wedge.

GRAPE & CHERI-BERI SNOW CONES

1 oz. DeKuyper Grape Pucker

1 oz. Cheri-Beri Pucker

Serve over crushed ice.

GRAPPLER

¾ oz. DeKuyper Sour
       Apple Pucker

¾ oz. DeKuyper Grape
       Pucker

       Soda water

Serve over ice.

GRASSHOPPER

½ oz. DeKuyper Green
       Crème de Menthe

½ oz. DeKuyper White
       Crème de Cacao

½ oz. Cream

Blend and serve in a wine
glass.

GREEN HORNET

½ oz. Vox Vodka

¼ oz. DeKuyper Melon
       Liqueur

½ oz. Sweet & Sour Mix

Shake with ice; serve straight
up or over ice.

GREEN LIZARD

1 part Chartreuse

1 part Bacardi 151 Rum

1 part Rose's Lime Juice

Layer this drink by pouring
Chartreuse first, then the
Rum, and then the Lime Juice.

GREEN MONDAY

1½ oz. Cointreau

        Mint leaves

        Lemon-lime soda

Fill a tumbler glass with
crushed ice and mint leaves.
Pour Cointreau over ice and
fill with lemon-lime soda.

GREEN SNEAKER

1 oz. Vox Vodka

½ oz. DeKuyper Melon
Liqueur

½ oz. Cointreau

2 oz. Orange Juice

Stir with ice, strain, and serve
straight up.

GREMLIN

1½ oz. Vox Vodka

¾ oz. DeKuyper Blue
Curacao

¾ oz. Bacardi Rum

½ oz. Orange Juice

Shake with ice, strain, and
serve straight up.

GREYHOUND

1½ oz. Vox Vodka

Grapefruit Juice

Pour Vox Vodka over crushed
ice in a tall glass. Fill with
Grapefruit Juice.

GREYHOUND MARTINI

2 parts Vox Vodka

4 parts Ruby Red Grapefruit
Juice

Shake ingredients with ice and
strain into glass.

GRIT COCKTAIL

1 oz. Tullamore Dew
Irish Whiskey

1 oz. Martini & Rossi
Dry Vermouth

Shake and then strain into
shot glass or serve over ice.

GUNRUNNER

½ oz. Drambuie

½ oz. Dewar's Scotch

1½ oz. Disaronno Amaretto

1 Tbs. Bacardi Rum

Shake with ice, strain over ice in a tall glass.

GUNGA DIN MARTINI

3 parts Bombay Sapphire Gin

1 part Martini & Rossi Dry Vermouth

Juice of ¼ Orange

Shake with ice. Garnish with a Pineapple Slice.

GYPSY MARTINI

1½ oz. Vox Vodka or Bombay Sapphire Gin

dash Martini & Rossi Extra Dry Vermouth

Shake with ice; serve straight up or on ice. Garnish with a Maraschino Cherry.

GYPSY'S KISS

1 part Irish Mist

1 part Orange Juice

1 part Lemon Juice or Sour Mix

Combine in a highball glass. You can also add a dash of Rose's Grenadine.

HALF & HALF MARTINI

3 parts Bombay Sapphire Gin

3 parts Vox Vodka

1 part Martini & Rossi Dry Vermouth

Shake with ice; serve straight up or on ice. Garnish with a Lemon Twist.

HARD HAT

1¼ oz. Bacardi Rum

1¼ oz. Fresh Lime Juice

1 tsp. Sugar

¼ oz. Rose's Grenadine

Club Soda

In a shaker with ice, combine all but the Club Soda. Stir and strain into a glass with ice. Fill with Club Soda.

HARVARD COCKTAIL

2 oz. Hennessy Cognac

1 oz. Martini & Rossi Rosso Vermouth

1 oz. Lemon Juice

1 tsp. Rose's Grenadine

1 dash Bitters

Shake with ice and strain into a cocktail glass.

HARVEY WALLBANGER

¼ oz. Liquore Galliano

1 oz. Vox Vodka

¾ full Orange Juice

In a tall glass with ice, add Vox Vodka and fill the glass with Orange Juice. Float the Galliano on top.

HAVANA SIDECAR

1½ oz. Bacardi Rum

¾ oz. Lemon Juice

¾ oz. Cointreau

Mix with ice and serve on ice.

HAWAIIAN COCKTAIL MARTINI

2 oz. Bombay Sapphire Gin

½ oz. Cointreau

½ oz. Unsweetened pineapple juice

Shake and strain.

HAWAIIAN NIGHT

1 oz. Bacardi Light Rum

¼ oz. DeKuyper Cherry-flavored Brandy

Pineapple juice

Pour rum into a tall glass half filled with ice. Fill with pineapple juice and float cherry-flavored brandy on top.

HAZELNUT COFFEE

B & B and Hazelnut Liqueur with coffee and whipped cream.

HENNESSY CONTINENTAL

1 oz. Hennessy Cognac

splash Cointreau

1½ oz. Cranberry Juice

½ oz. Grapefruit Juice

Strain into a chilled martini glass.

HENNESSY CHOCOLATE MARTINI

2 oz. Hennessy Cognac

1 oz. DeKuyper Creme de Cacao

Shake with ice.

HENNESSY SOUR

1 oz. Hennessy VS

1 oz. Sour mix

Shake with ice. Pour into snifter glass.

HIGH VOLTAGE

½ oz. Lime or lemon juice

½ oz. Cointreau

1 oz. Dewar's Scotch

Pour lime or lemon juice, Cointreau and Dewar's into an old-fashioned glass with ice: Fill with soda water. Stir.

HOME RUN

1 oz. Knob Creek Bourbon

½ oz. Bacardi Light Rum

1 oz. Hennessy Cognac

2 tsp. Lemon Juice

Shake with ice and serve over ice.

HONOLULU HURRICANE MARTINI

4 parts Bombay Sapphire Gin

1 part Martini & Rossi Dry Vermouth

1 part Martini & Rossi Rosso Vermouth

1 tsp. Pineapple juice

Shake and strain into martini glass.

HOP-SKIP-AND-GO NAKED

1 oz. Vox Vodka

1 oz. Bombay Sapphire Gin

Juice of ½ Lime

In a mug; serve over ice. Fill with Budweiser.

HORNY BULL

1¼ oz. Jose Cuervo Tequila

Orange Juice

Add Cuervo to a chilled highball glass filled with ice. Fill with Orange Juice.

HORSESHOT

1¼ oz. Vox Vodka

4 oz. Tomato Juice

1¼ tsp. Horseradish

Over ice in a cocktail glass. Garnish with celery stalk or tomato slice.

HOT APPLE

3 oz. Laird's Applejack

3 oz. Hot Cider or Apple Juice

Pour into a thick tumbler or mug. Twist and drop in a spiral of lemon peel, dust with powdered cinnamon or cinnamon stick.

HOT APPLE PIE

¾ oz. DeKuyper Sour Apple Pucker

¼ oz. DeKuyper Hot Damn!

Fill with hot apple cider, garnish with a cinnamon stick.

HOT APPLE RUM

¾ oz. DeKuyper Sour
        Apple Pucker

¾ oz. Bacardi Rum

5 oz. Hot water

2 tsp. Butter

Sprinkle with cinnamon and
serve in a mug.

HOT BUTTERED COMFORT

1 jigger Southern Comfort

small Stick cinnamon

        Slice lemon peel

        Pat butter

Float butter. Stir. Serve in a
coffee cup or mug.

HOT APPLE TODDY

¾ oz. DeKuyper Sour
        Apple Pucker

¾ oz. DeKuyper Thrilla
        Vanilla

6 oz. Hot apple
        cider/juice

Serve in a mug.

HOT IRISH

1½ oz. Tullamore Dew Irish
         Whiskey

2 tsp. Sugar (brown if
         available)

½ slice Fresh Lemon

4 Cloves

pinch Cinnamon

         Boiling Water

Stud the Lemon Slice with
Cloves. Put Lemon, Sugar, and
Cinnamon into a warm glass.
Add Boiling Water and Irish
Whiskey. Stir well and serve in
a mug or coffee cup.

HOT MIST

2 parts Irish Mist

1 part Boiling Water

Combine in the glass and garnish with a slice of Lemon and some cloves.

HOT MULLED

2 oz. Dewar's 12 Year Old

Serve with a splash of hot water.

HOT TODDY

2 oz. Knob Creek Bourbon

1 tsp. Sugar

Boiling water

Serve in mug. Garnish with lemon slice and dust with nutmeg or add cinnamon stick.

HULA HOOP

1½ oz. Vox Vodka

2 oz. Pineapple Juice

½ oz. Orange Juice

Combine over ice.

ILLUSION

1 oz. Cointreau

½ oz. Bacardi Rum

½ oz. DeKuyper Melon Liqueur

½ oz. Vox Vodka

2 oz. Pineapple Juice

Serve in tall glass with ice.

IMPERIAL

1¼ oz. Knob Creek Bourbon

splash Club Soda

1¼ oz. Cointreau

splash Simple Syrup

1 scoop Crushed Ice

Mix together all the ingredients except the Club Soda in a shaker. Strain the mixture into a rocks glass over ice. Top off the glass with Club Soda.

INOCULATION SHOT

1 oz. Jose Cuervo Gold Tequila

¼ oz. DeKuyper Blue Curacao

Shake with ice and strain into a shot glass.

IRISH ANGEL

¾ oz. Tullamore Dew Irish Whiskey

¼ oz. DeKuyper White Creme de Cacao

¼ oz. DeKuyper White Creme de Menthe

1½ oz. Heavy cream

Shake and serve in a martini glass.

IRISH APPLE

2 parts Carolans Irish Cream

1 part Laird's Apple Jack

Stir.

IRISH BUCK

1½ oz. Tullamore Dew Irish Whiskey

Ginger Ale

Pour Tullamore Dew Irish Whiskey into chilled highball glass with cracked ice. Twist a Lemon Peel over the drink and drop it in. Fill with Ginger Ale.

IRISH CANADIAN

½ oz. Irish Mist

1½ oz. Canadian Whiskey

Stir well and serve.

IRISH CELEBRATION

1¼ oz. Tullamore Dew Irish Whiskey

¼ oz. DeKuyper Green Creme de Menthe

splash Champagne

Shake; top with Champagne.

IRISH CHARLIE

1 part Carolans Irish Cream

1 part DeKuyper White Crème de Menthe

Shake with ice and strain into a shot glass. You can also layer the Irish Cream over the Crème de Menthe.

IRISH COFFEE

Into a stemmed glass, put 2 tsp. sugar, preferably brown; add ⅓ Tullamore Dew Irish Whiskey and ⅔ really strong black coffee, preferably freshly brewed, not instant. The glass should be filled with this mixture to within half an inch of the brim. Stir well at this point to ensure all of the sugar is dissolved, and then carefully float over the back of a spoon a collar of lightly-whipped cream, so that the cream floats on the top of the coffee and whiskey. Do not stir any more. Serve the drink without a spoon or a straw, as part of the pleasure comes from sipping the hot coffee and whiskey through the cool cream.

It's Ray Foley's favorite.

IRISH COFFEE (SIMPLE)

Tullamore Dew Irish Whiskey, hot coffee, sugar, whipped cream.

IRISH COOLER

1¼ oz. Tullamore Dew

6 oz. Club soda

Garnish with a lemon peel spiral.

IRISH COW

1½ oz. Tullamore Dew Irish Whiskey

8 oz. Hot Milk

1 tsp. Sugar

Pour the Milk into a glass. Add the Sugar and Whiskey. Stir well.

IRISH COWBOY

1 part Carolans Irish
Cream

1 part Knob Creek
Bourbon

Shake and serve over ice.

IRISH DELIGHT

1½ oz. Tullamore Dew Irish
Whiskey

¾ oz. Cream

Stir and serve.

IRISH CREAM STINGER

3 parts Carolans Irish
Cream

1 part DeKuyper White
Crème de Menthe

Stir well over ice.

IRISH DREAM

½ oz. Carolans Irish
Cream

½ oz. DeKuyper Hazelnut
Liqueur

½ oz. DeKuyper Dark
Creme de Cacao

1 scoop Vanilla ice cream

Blend and serve.

IRISH CUP O' JOE

Carolans Irish Cream,
chocolate syrup, hot coffee.

How sweet it is!

IRISH EYES

1 oz. Tullamore Dew
       Irish Whiskey

¼ oz. DeKuyper Green
       Crème de Menthe

2 oz. Heavy Cream

Shake well with crushed
ice. Strain into a chilled
cocktail glass. Garnish with
Maraschino Cherry.

IRISH FIX

2 oz. Tullamore Dew Irish
       Whiskey

½ oz. Irish Mist

1 oz. Pineapple Juice

½ oz. Lemon Juice

½ tsp. Sugar Syrup

Fill mixing glass with ice.
Combine ingredients and stir.

IRISH FROST SHOOTER

1 shot Carolans Irish
        Cream

1 splash Coco Lopez Cream
          of Coconut

1 splash Half & Half

Shake and strain. Garnish
with Cinnamon.

IRISH HEADLOCK

¼ oz. Carolans Irish
       Cream

¼ oz. Tullamore Dew Irish
       Whiskey

¼ oz. Disaronno Amaretto

¼ oz. Brandy

Layer in above order.

IRISH KISS

¾ oz. Tullamore Dew Irish Whiskey

½ oz. DeKuyper Peachtree Schnapps

4 oz. Ginger Ale

2 oz. Orange Juice

Combine ingredients in an ice cube-filled collins glass. Garnish with a Lime Wheel.

IRISH KNIGHT

2 oz. Tullamore Dew Irish Whiskey

2 oz. Martini & Rossi Dry Vermouth

2 dashes Benedictine

Combine in a rocks glass with ice. Add a twist of Orange Peel.

IRISH KNIT

1 oz. Carolans Irish Cream

1 oz. Cointreau

Hot coffee

Serve in a warm mug.

IRISH LACED

1 shot Irish Mist

2 splashes Coco Lopez Cream of Coconut

2 splashes Half & half

3 splashes Pineapple juice

2 scoops Ice

Blend. Serve in a tall glass.

IRISH MAGIC

1 oz.   Tullamore Dew Irish Whiskey

¼ oz.   DeKuyper White Crème de Cacao

5 oz.   Orange Juice

Pour all ingredients over ice in a glass. Stir.

IRISH MIST ALEXANDER

1 oz.   Irish Mist

1 oz.   Light Cream

1 oz.   DeKuyper Dark Crème de Cacao

Shake ingredients with cracked ice and strain. Sprinkle with Nutmeg.

IRISH MIST COFFEE

Hot coffee

1½ oz.   Irish Mist

Top with whipped cream.

IRISH MIST KISS

1 part   Irish Mist

dash   DeKuyper Blue Curacao

splash   Soda

Serve in a rocks glass over ice.

IRISH MIST SODA

1 part   Irish Mist

3 parts   Club Soda

Serve with ice and a wedge of Lime or Lemon in a tall glass.

IRISH NIGHT CAP

1½ oz. Tullamore Dew Irish
Whiskey

4 oz. Hot milk

1 tsp. Sugar

Stir.

IRISH PENANCE

1 part Carolans Irish
Cream

1 part Cointreau

Shake slowly and serve on the
rocks.

IRISH PRINCE

1¼ oz. Tullamore Dew Irish
Whiskey

3 oz. Tonic water

Stir.

IRISH RICKEY

1½ oz. Tullamore Dew
Irish Whiskey

1 cube Ice

juice of ½ lime

Fill 8 oz. highball glass with
carbonated water and stir.
Leave lime in glass.

IRISH ROSE HIGHBALL

1 jigger Tullamore Dew
Irish Whiskey

⅓ jigger Rose's Grenadine

Club Soda

Combine first two ingredients
in a glass and fill with Club
Soda.

IRISH RUSSIAN

1 part Carolans Irish
Cream

1 part Vox Vodka

Stir.

IRISH SHILLELAGH

1½ oz. Tullamore Dew Irish Whiskey

½ oz. DeKuyper Sloe Gin

½ oz. Bacardi Light Rum

1 oz. Lemon Juice

1 tsp. Sugar Syrup

2 Peach Slices, diced

Mix all ingredients with cracked ice in a shaker or blend. Pour into a chilled rocks glass. Garnish with Raspberries and a Maraschino Cherry.

IRISH SLING

1 oz. Tullamore Dew Irish Whiskey

1 oz. Bombay Sapphire Gin

1 lump Sugar

Crush Sugar with ice in a glass. Add Tullamore Dew and Gin and Stir.

IRISH SOUR

1½ oz. Tullamore Dew Irish Whiskey

1 tsp. Sugar

Juice of ½ Lemon

Shake vigorously with ice until frothy. Stir into sour glass. Add a Maraschino Cherry and an Orange Slice.

IRISH SPRING

1 oz. Tullamore Dew Irish Whiskey

½ oz. DeKuyper Peachtree Schnapps

1 oz. Orange Juice

1 oz. Sweet and sour mix

In a Collins glass with ice, stir well. Garnish with orange slice and Maraschino cherry.

IRISH STING

1½ oz. Tullamore Dew Irish
        Whiskey

¼ oz. DeKuyper White
       Crème de Menthe

Shake. Serve straight up or
over ice.

IRISH SUMMER COFFEE

1 oz. Tullamore Dew Irish
       Whiskey

¼ oz. Carolans Irish
       Cream

4 oz. Cold Coffee

       Whipped Cream

Stir first three ingredients
with ice and strain. Top with
Whipped Cream if desired.

IRISH SURFER

1¼ oz. Irish Mist

3 oz. Orange juice

       Sugar

       Club soda

Shake Irish Mist, orange juice
and sugar. Top with club soda.

ISLAND ECSTASY

2 parts DeKuyper Tropical
         Pineapple

1 part Vox Vodka

splash Rose's Grenadine

Fill with orange juice. Serve
over ice in a tall glass.

ISLAND TEA

1½ oz. Vox Vodka

1 oz. Rose's Grenadine

1 tsp. Lemon Juice

Combine with ice and shake.
Strain over ice in a rocks glass
and garnish with a Mint
Sprig.

ITALIAN APPLE COFFEE

¾ oz. DeKuyper Sour Apple Pucker

¾ oz. Disaronno Amaretto

6 oz. Fresh coffee

Serve in a mug.

ITALIAN COLADA

¼ oz. Coco Lopez Cream of Coconut

1½ oz. Bacardi Light Rum

¼ oz. Disaronno Amaretto

¾ oz. Sweet Cream

2 oz. Pineapple Juice

Blend.

ITALIAN DREAM

1½ oz. Carolans Irish Cream

½ oz. Disaronno Amaretto

2 oz. Half & half

4 oz. Ice cubes

Blend.

ITALIAN ICED TEA

1 oz. Martini & Rossi Rosso Vermouth

3 oz. Gingerale

Add ingredients to a tall glass with ice. Garnish with an orange slice.

ITALIAN MARTINI

1½ oz. Vox Vodka or
        Bombay Sapphire
        Gin

dash Disaronno Amaretto

Stir with ice. Serve on ice or
strain.

ITALIAN MANHATTAN

½ oz. Disaronno Amaretto

¼ oz. Maraschino Cherry
        Juice

1½ oz. Knob Creek
         Bourbon

Cocktail glass, chilled or rocks
glass, add ice, stir and garnish
with an orange slice and a
cherry.

ITALIAN WHITE SANGRIA

1 750ml bottle Martini &
         Rossi Extra Dry
         Vermouth

1 cup Cointreau

1 cup Juice of three
       oranges

½ cup Juice of two lemons

¼ cup Juice of one lime

½ cup Sugar

1 Orange, halved and
   thinly sliced

1 Lemon, halved and
   thinly sliced

1 Apple, cored and
   thinly sliced

1 cup Chilled sparkling
       water

Combine Martini & Rossi
Extra Dry Vermouth,
Cointreau, fruit juices and
sugar is large pitcher. Stir until
the sugar is dissolved. Chill
until ready to serve. Stir in
sliced fruit and sparkling
water; serve over ice. Makes
7 cups.

J.J.'S SHAMROCK

1 oz. Tullamore Dew Irish Whiskey

½ oz. DeKuyper White Crème de Cacao

½ oz. DeKuyper Green Crème de Menthe

1 oz. Milk

Mix in a shaker or blender with cracked ice and serve in a chilled glass.

JACK ROSE

1½ oz. Laird's Applejack

¾ oz. Sour Mix

tsp. Rose's Grenadine

Shake with ice. Strain.

JACK ROSE COCKTAIL

2 oz. Laird's Applejack

1 oz. Lemon Juice

½ oz. Grenadine

Shake well with ice and strain into cocktail glass or serve over ice.

JADE

1½ oz. Bacardi Light Rum

¾ oz. Lime juice

1 barsp. Sugar

dash Cointreau

dash DeKuyper Green Crème de Menthe

Shake with ice and serve over ice.

JAMAICAN DUST

1 part Bacardi Rum

1 part Tia Maria

1 part Pineapple Juice

Shake with ice and strain into a shot glass.

JAMIE'S HIGHLAND SPECIAL

1 part DeKuyper Green
Crème de Menthe

1 part Galliano

1 part DeKuyper
Blackberry Liqueur

1 part Kirschwasser

Layer this drink in the order listed. Start with Crème de Menthe on the bottom and finish Kirschwasser on top.

JAPANESE SLIPPER

1 oz. Cointreau

$\frac{1}{2}$ oz. DeKuyper Melon
Liqueur

$\frac{1}{2}$ oz. Lemon

Shake. Serve on the rocks or straight up.

JASMINE

$\frac{1}{2}$ oz. Cointreau

1 oz. Bombay Sapphire
Gin

$\frac{1}{2}$ oz. Campari

2 oz. Lemon Juice

Shake with ice. Serve up or on the rocks.

JELLY BEAN

1 part DeKuyper Anisette

1 part DeKuyper
Blackberry-Flavored
Brandy

You can strain this one into a shot glass or serve on the rocks.

JELLY BEAN II

1 part DeKuyper
Peppermint
Schnapps

1 part DeKuyper
Blackberry Brandy

You can strain or serve this one also on the rocks.

JELLYFISH

1 part Carolans Irish
Cream

1 part DeKuyper White
Crème de Cacao

1 part Disaronno Amaretto

1 part Rose's Grenadine

Pour first three ingredients directly into the glass. Pour Rose's Grenadine in the center of the glass.

JERSEY BOUNCE

1½ oz. Laird's Applejack

dash Cointreau

dash Rose's Lime Juice

1½ oz. Sour Mix

1½ oz. Cranberry Juice

dash Egg White, if desired

Shake well and garnish with wedge of lime.

JERSEY DEVIL

1½ oz. Laird's Applejack

½ oz. Cointreau

½ tsp. Sugar

½ oz. Rose's Lime Juice

½ oz. Cranberry Juice

Shake well with ice and strain into cocktail glass.

JOCOSE JULEP

½ oz. Knob Creek Bourbon

½ oz. DeKuyper Green Creme de Menthe

1 oz. Lime Juice

1 tsp. Sugar

5 Chopped Mint Leaves

Club Soda

Combine all ingredients except club soda in blender without ice. Pour into collins glass over ice cubes. Fill with club soda and decorate with a sprig of mint.

JOHN COLLINS

1 oz. Knob Creek Bourbon

½ oz. Sugar Syrup

Juice of ½ Lime

Club Soda

Pour Lemon Juice, Syrup, and Bourbon in a highball glass filled with ice. Squeeze in the Juice from ½ Lime and save the shell. Fill the glass with Club Soda. Stir.

JOLLEE-RANCHER

1 oz. DeKuyper Peachtree Schnapps

½ oz. DeKuyper Sour Apple Pucker

½ oz. Cranberry juice

Shake and serve over rocks.

JOLLY ROGER

½ oz. Drambuie

1½ oz. Bacardi Light Rum

1 oz. Fresh Lime Juice

¼ tsp. Dewar's Scotch

Sparkling Water

Combine all ingredients, except sparkling water, with cracked ice in a cocktail shaker. Shake well and pour into chilled highball glass. Fill with sparkling water and stir gently.

JOURNALIST MARTINI

1½ oz. Bombay Sapphire Gin

¼ oz. Martini & Rossi Rosso Vermouth

¼ oz. Martini & Rossi Dry Vermouth

1 dash Angostura bitters

1 dash Lemon Juice

1 dash DeKuyper Orange Curacao

Stir with ice. Serve over ice or strain.

JUICE FRUIT MARTINI

½ oz. Bombay Sapphire Gin

½ oz. Cointreau

squeeze Lemon

splash Orange Juice

Serve chilled, straight up with lemon twist.

The Parish Cafe
Boston, MA

JUICY FRUIT

1 part Vox Vodka

1 part DeKuyper Peachtree Schnapps

1 part DeKuyper Melon Liqueur

1 part Pineapple Juice

Shake with ice and strain into a shot glass.

KAMIKAZI

1 oz. Vox Vodka

½ oz. Cointreau

¼ oz. Rose's Lime Juice

Shake with ice and strain into a shot glass.

KENTUCKY BLIZZARD

1½ oz. Knob Creek Bourbon

2 oz. Cranberry Juice

½ oz. Lime Juice

1 tsp. Sugar

Shake all ingredients with cracked ice. Strain into cocktail glass or over fresh cracked ice in old-fashioned glass. Garnish with a half-slice of orange.

KENTUCKY COCKTAIL

1½ oz. Knob Creek Bourbon

1 oz. Pineapple Juice

Shake with ice and strain into a cocktail glass.

KENTUCKY COLONEL COCKTAIL

1½ oz. Knob Creek Bourbon

½ oz. Benedictine

Stir with ice; strain into cocktail glass. Add a twist of lemon.

KEY LIME HIGH

½ oz. Cointreau

½ oz. Liquore Galliano

½ oz. Orange Juice

splash Lime

splash Half & Half

Shake with ice and strain. Makes two.

KEY WEST MARTINI

1 oz. Vox Vodka

½ oz. Bacardi Cóco

½ oz. DeKuyper Melon Liqueur

½ oz. DeKuyper Peachtree Schnapps

½ oz. Cranberry juice

Shake with ice and strain into martini glass.

KILLER KOOL-AID

1 part Chambord

1 part Vox Vodka

1 part Bombay Sapphire Gin

1 part Bacardi Light Rum

2 oz. Cranberry Juice

1 oz. Sour Mix

Combine in a tall glass over ice.

KILTED BLACK LEPRECHAUN

½ oz. Drambuie

1 oz. Carolans Irish Cream

½ oz. Bacardi Light Rum

Shake with ice. Strain. Serve as a shot.

KILTLIFTER

1 oz. Drambuie

1 oz. Dewar's Scotch

splash Rose's Lime Juice

Shake with ice. Serve over rocks.

KING ALPHONSE

1 part DeKuyper Dark
Crème de Cacao

1 part Cream

Layer the Cream on top of the DeKuyper Dark Crème de Cacao.

KIR OR KIR ROYALE

3 oz. Champagne

splash DeKuyper Crème de Cassis

Fill the glass with Champagne and add a splash of Crème de Cassis.

KNOB CREEK BOURBON SLING

2 oz. Knob Creek
Bourbon

1 tsp. Superfine Sugar

2 tsp. Water

1 oz. Lemon Juice

Shake well. Strain into a glass. Top with a Lemon Twist.

KNOB CREEK BOURBON STREET

1½ oz. Knob Creek
Bourbon

½ oz. Disaronno Amaretto

Shake with ice and strain into a shot glass.

KNUCKLE-BUSTER (AKA KNUCKLE-DUSTER)

½ oz. Drambuie

1½ oz. Dewar's Scotch

1 tsp. Bacardi 151 Rum

In an old-fashioned glass, pour over ice. Stir.

LA BOMBA

1¼ oz. Jose Cuervo 1800 Tequila

¾ oz. Cointreau

1½ oz. Pineapple Juice

1½ oz. Orange Juice

2 dashes Rose's Grenadine

Pour into glass and add Rose's Grenadine. Garnish with a Lime Wheel.

LA JOLLARITA

1½ oz. Jose Cuervo Traditional Tequila

½ oz. Cointreau

½ oz. Chambord

Shake, strain, and serve.

LADIES' CHOICE MARTINI

1½ oz. Vox Vodka

dash Martini & Rossi Extra Dry Vermouth

¼ oz. Kummel

Stir with ice and strain.

LADY SCARLETT

½ oz. Cointreau

1 oz. Bombay Sapphire Gin

¼ oz. Martini & Rossi Dry Vermouth

¼ oz. Lime Juice

dash Bitters

Shake with ice. Serve over ice.

LASER DISK

½ oz. Drambuie

½ oz. Dewar's Scotch

½ oz. Lemonade

Shake. Serve in shot glass.

LEAP FROG

1 oz. Bacardi O™

1 oz. Cointreau

1½ oz. Sweet & Sour Mix

½ oz. Fresh-squeezed Orange Juice

Shake; garnish with lime and two Maraschino cherries on each end of lime (the frog).

LEMON CHIFFON

½ oz. Cointreau

1 oz. Vox Vodka

1 oz. Sweet & Sour Mix

Shake ingredients with ice and serve over ice. Squeeze and drop in a fresh lemon wedge.

LEMON ICE

1¼ oz. Vox Vodka

½ oz. Cointreau

1½ oz. Sweet & Sour Mix

½ oz. Lemon Juice

Build over ice and fill with 7-Up in a 10 oz. glass. Garnish with a Lemon Slice.

LEPRECHAUN

2 oz. Tullamore Dew Irish Whiskey

3 oz. Tonic water

3-4 Ice cubes

twist Lemon peel

Stir gently. Drop in lemon peel.

LICORICE STICK

1 part Cointreau

1 part Vox Vodka

1 part DeKuyper Anisette

Shake with ice and strain into a shot glass.

LIFESAVER

1 part Bacardi Rum

1 part Vox Vodka

1 part DeKuyper Melon Liqueur

1 part 7-Up

Shake with ice and strain into a shot glass.

LIME ISLAND ICED TEA

3 oz. Vox Vodka

1½ oz. Cointreau

4 oz. Iced tea

2 Tbs. Rose's Lime Juice

Combine iced tea, Vox Vodka, Cointreau and lime juice, shake and strain into a collins glass filled with ice.

LIMESTONE

2 oz. Knob Creek Bourbon

1½ oz. Collins Mix/Lemon Juice

splash Lime Juice

Into ice-filled highball glass, pour Bourbon, fill glass with collins mix; add lime juice.

LIMÓN & CRANBERRY

1 part Bacardi Limón

4 parts Cranberry juice

Pour ingredients over ice in a rocks glass. Garnish with lemon twist.

LIMÓN BAYBREEZE

1½ oz. Bacardi Limón

2 oz. Cranberry juice

2 oz. Pineapple juice

Pour Limón into tall glass with ice. Fill with equal parts cranberry and pineapple juice. Garnish with a pineapple wedge.

LIMÓN COSMO

2 oz. Bacardi Limón

½ oz. Cointreau

½ oz. Lime juice

2 oz. Cranberry juice

Shake with ice, strain into a chilled martini glass.

LIMÓN SEABREEZE

1½ oz. Bacardi Limón

2 oz. Cranberry juice

2 oz. Grapefruit juice

Pour Limón into tall glass with ice. Fill with equal parts cranberry and grapefruit juice.

LIPSMACKER

2 oz. DeKuyper Cheri-Beri Pucker

½ oz. Rose's Lime Juice

splash Club Soda

Serve over ice.

LITTLE DEVIL

drop Tabasco

Lemon slice

drop Worcestershire sauce

½ oz. Lime or lemon juice

½ oz. Cointreau

1 oz. Bombay Sapphire Gin

Tomato juice

Pour all ingredients (except tomato juice) into a tumbler glass with ice. Fill with tomato juice. Stir.

LIZARD SLIME

1½ oz. Jose Cuervo Mistico Tequila

½ oz. DeKuyper Melon Liqueur

In a shot glass, float the DeKuyper on top of the Cuervo.

LOCH LOMOND

½ oz. Drambuie

1 oz. Dewar's Scotch

½ oz. Martini & Rossi Dry
Vermouth

1 Lemon Twist

In a mixing glass half filled
with ice, combine the Dewar's,
Drambuie, and Martini &
Rossi Vermouth. Stir well.
Strain into a cocktail glass.
Garnish with the lemon twist.

LOUISVILLE COOLER

1½ oz. Knob Creek
Bourbon

2 oz. Orange Juice

1 Tbs. Lime Juice

1 tsp. Powdered Sugar

Shake all ingredients with
cracked ice. Strain into old-
fashioned glass over crushed
ice. Garnish with orange
wheel.

LONG ISLAND ICED TEA

½ oz. Vox Vodka

½ oz. Bacardi Rum

½ oz. Bombay Dry Gin

½ oz. Cointreau

½ oz. Jose Cuervo Tequila

Cola

Shake the first five ingredients
over ice and strain into a
glass. Fill with Cola.

LOUISVILLE LADY

1¼ oz. Knob Creek
Bourbon

¾ oz. DeKuyper White
Creme de Cacao

1 oz. Cream

Shake and strain into cocktail
glass.

LOVER'S KISS

1 oz.   Disaronno Amaretto

½ oz.   DeKuyper Cherry
        Brandy

½ oz.   DeKuyper Dark
        Creme de Cacao

1 oz.   Cream or Half &
        Half

Shake with ice. Strain into a
chilled martini glass. Garnish
with a maraschino cherry.

LUCK OF
THE IRISH

2 oz.   Carolans Irish
        Cream Liqueur

2 oz.   Tullamore Dew
        Irish Whiskey

1 oz.   Irish Mist

Shake.

LUCKY BOY

½ oz.   Lime juice

2 oz.   Grapefruit juice

1½ oz. Cointreau

        Soda water

        Mint cordial

Shake lime juice, grapefruit
juice and Cointreau with ice.
Strain into a tumbler glass
with ice. Fill with soda water.
Add a drop of mint cordial.
Stir. Garnish with lime slice
and a Maraschino cherry.

LUCKY LADY

¾ oz.   Bacardi Light Rum

¼ oz.   DeKuyper Anisette

¼ oz.   DeKuyper White
        Crème de Cacao

¾ oz.   Cream

Blend with crushed ice and
serve in a margarita glass.

MACARENA

1 oz. Jose Cuervo Especial Tequila

½ oz. Bacardi Cóco

3 oz. Sweet & Sour Mix

1 oz. Orange Juice

1 oz. Pineapple Juice

splash Cranberry Juice

Shake and pour over ice into a tall glass. Garnish with Pineapple, Orange, and a Maraschino Cherry.

MAD MARTINI

1 part DeKuyper Mad Melon Watermelon

2 parts Vox Vodka

splash Lime juice

Garnish with a lemon twist.

MAD PUCKER

⅔ oz. DeKuyper Mad Melon Watermelon

⅓ oz. DeKuyper Sour Apple Pucker

Shake. Strain into shot glass.

MADRAS

1¼ oz. Vox Vodka

2 oz. Cranberry Juice

2 oz. Orange Juice

Pour Vox Vodka over ice in a tall glass. Fill half way with Orange Juice and top it off with Cranberry Juice.

MAGNOLIA MAIDEN

1¼ oz. Knob Creek Bourbon

1¼ oz. Cointreau

1 splash Simple Syrup

1 splash Club Soda

Shake Bourbon, Cointreau, and simple syrup. Strain into glass with ice. Top with club soda.

MAI TAI

¾ oz. Bacardi Light Rum

¼ oz. Bacardi 151 Rum

½ oz. DeKuyper Orange Curacao

½ oz. Rose's Lime Juice

¼ oz. Orgeat Syrup

¼ oz. Simple Syrup

Stir with ice. Garnish with Mint, Maraschino Cherry, and Pineapple.

MAIDEN'S PRAYER

2 parts Bombay Dry Gin

2 parts Cointreau

1 part Orange Juice

1 part Lemon Juice

Shake with ice and strain into a glass.

MAIDEN'S PRAYER II

½ oz. Cointreau

1 oz. Bombay Sapphire Gin

½ oz. Bacardi Light Rum

2 oz. Lemon Juice

Shake with ice. Serve over ice or up.

MAIN SQUEEZE

1½ oz. DeKuyper Wild Strawberry Liqueur

2 oz. Cranberry Juice

2 oz. Orange Juice

Club Soda

Combine first three ingredients in a tall glass and top with Club Soda.

MANGO FROZEN MARGARITA

1½ parts Jose Cuervo Especial

3 parts Jose Cuervo Margarita Mix

1 cup Diced, peeled ripe Mango

1 ½ Tbs. Superfine Granulated Sugar

1 cup Ice Cubes

Blend all ingredients in a blender until smooth. Pour into margarita glass.

MANHATTAN

2 oz. Knob Creek Bourbon

splash Martini & Rossi Rosso or Dry Vermouth

dash Angostura Bitters

Stir. Garnish with a Maraschino Cherry.

MARASCHINO

1½ oz. Bombay Sapphire Gin

½ oz. Maraschino Cherry Juice

Shake. Strain drink into a cocktail glass.

MARGARITA

1 part Jose Cuervo Especial

2 parts Sweet and Sour Mix

1 part Lime Juice

splash Cointreau

Salt on the rim of the glass.

Shake and serve on the rocks!

MARGARITA MADRES

1¼ oz. Jose Cuervo Gold Tequila

½ oz. Cointreau

1½ oz. Sweet & Sour Mix

1½ oz. Orange Juice

1½ oz. Cranberry Juice

Blend with crushed ice. Serve in a tall glass. Garnish with a Lime.

MARGARITA PERFECT CUERVO

1½ parts Jose Cuervo Especial

3 parts Jose Cuervo Margarita Mix

½ cup Crushed Ice

Salt

Lime Wedge

Mix all ingredients (except salt and lime) in a blender. Rub the rims of a margarita glass with lime and then dip into salt to frost. Pour into glass and garnish with lime wedge.

MARGARITA SPRITZER

1½ parts Jose Cuervo Especial

3 parts Jose Cuervo Margarita Mix

Chilled Seltzer or Club Soda

1 Lime Slice

In a Margarita glass, combine Jose Cuervo Especial, Jose Cuervo Margarita Mix and four ice cubes. Fill the glass with the seltzer and stir the drink. Garnish with the lime slice.

MARTINI

2 oz. Bombay Sapphire Gin

dash Martini & Rossi Extra Dry Vermouth

Shake or stir Bombay Sapphire Gin and Vermouth over ice. Strain and serve in a cocktail glass straight up or over ice. Garnish with a Twist or an Olive.

MARTINI BELLINI

2 oz. Vox Vodka or Bombay Sapphire Gin

¼ oz. DeKuyper Peachtree Schnapps

Shake or stir Vox Vodka or Bombay Sapphire Gin and DeKuyper Peachtree Schnapps over ice. Strain and serve.

MARY PICKFORD

1½ oz. Bacardi Light Rum

1½ oz. Pineapple Juice

1 splash Rose's Grenadine

Shake with crushed ice. Serve over ice or strain.

Presenting VOX® Raspberry

An Irresistible Act of Smoothness

Experience the exceptionally smooth taste and vibrant clarity of VOX® Vodka in a delicious new way. VOX® Raspberry flavored vodka will excite your senses with an alluring aroma and tantalizing taste created from the essence of fresh raspberries.

To best appreciate this seductive spirit, serve straight up and deeply chilled or poured gently over ice. VOX® Raspberry sets a new standard for flavored spirits and lifts any martini to a new level of taste and drinkability.

The Experts Have Fallen for VOX® Raspberry

"★★★★⸱"

"Much fruitier, fresher, and fuller in taste
and texture (than the competition)."

Richard Carleton Hacker, Spirits Connoisseur (*Playboy, The Robb Report*)

"★★★★⸱"

"Possibly the finest raspberry flavored
spirit I've tried to-date."

-Robert Plotkin, Spirits Connoisseur (*Bar Media*)

Shake up
your
night

BACARDI

BACARDI
O
ORIGINAL ORANGE RUM
BACARDI RUM WITH NATURAL ORANGE FLAVOR

BACARDI
LIMÓN

BACARDI
VANÍLA
ORIGINAL VANILLA RUM
BACARDI RUM WITH NATURAL FLAVORS

BACARDI
CÓCO
ORIGINAL COCONUT RUM
BACARDI RUM WITH NATURAL FLAVORS

BACARDI
RAZZ
ORIGINAL RASPBERRY RUM
BACARDI RUM WITH NATURAL FLAVORS

CHAMBORD MARTINI
1/2 oz. Chambord   1 oz. Vodka   2 oz. Pineapple juice   Add lemon twist.

BE COINTREAUVERSIAL™
TO THE BEAT OF A DIFFERENT DRUM

the original margarita

1 part Cointreau®
2 parts tequila
fresh lime juice
shake well
pour over ice

Every pink drink needs a cherry in it or on it!

Aromatherapy.

By "marrying" our unique blend of 12 year old whiskies, we take an extra step in our aging process most other Scotches don't. This creates a Scotch with such perfectly balanced notes of caramel and spice, simply smelling it is considered a relaxation technique.

Dewar's

FINEST SCOTCH WHISKY

AGED **12** YEARS

Savor Every Detail.

THE PERFECT IRISH MIX

ese distinctive Irish brands are certain to bring life to your bar. Served neat as mixers in many popular and newly introduced cocktails, they are sure deliver your customers a wee taste o' Ireland right here at home.

r a FREE copy of our Preferred Food & Drink Recipes booklet featuring three Irish brands, e-mail us at carolans@hcaadvertising.com or visit r Web site at www.carolans.ie.

IT CONTROLS THE WEATHER* VIVE **Cuervo**

Hecho en México. Desde 1795.

*NOT TRUE. ONLY THE GOVERNMENT CAN DO THAT. DRINK RESPONSIBLY.

www.cuervo.com

MELON BALL

¾ oz. DeKuyper Melon
         Liqueur

1 oz. Vox Vodka

4 oz. Orange Juice

Combine in a glass and stir.

MELON CITRUS COOLER

1 part DeKuyper Pucker
         Watermelon
         Schnapps

1 part Vox Vodka

Fill with orange juice and
serve over ice.

MELONTINI

1 part DeKuyper Pucker
         Watermelon
         Schnapps

1 part Vox Vodka

splash Lemon-lime soda

Garnish with watermelon
slice.

MELORITA

1 part DeKuyper Pucker
         Watermelon
         Schnapps

1 part Jose Cuervo Tequila

2 parts Sweet & sour mix

Salt rim of glass and serve
over crushed ice.

METROPOLITAN

1 oz. Martini & Rossi
        Rosso Vermouth

2 oz. Hennessy Cognac

½ tsp. Sugar Syrup

2 dashes Angostura Bitters

4-5 Ice Cubes

Shake and strain into a chilled
martini glass.

MEXI-COLA

1 part Jose Cuervo Clásico

4 parts Cola Soda

Combine Cuervo and soda in a rocks glass with ice. Garnish with lime wedge.

MEXICAN BANANA

1½ oz. Jose Cuervo Tequila

¾ oz. DeKuyper Crème de Banana

Pour ingredients into a rocks-glass filled with ice.

MEXICAN BERRY

1 oz. Chambord

1 oz. Jose Cuervo Tequila

Shake with ice and strain into a shot glass.

MEXICAN PAIN KILLER

½ oz. Jose Cuervo Tequila

½ oz. Vox Vodka

½ oz. Bacardi Light Rum

1 oz. Pineapple Juice

½ oz. Orange Juice

2 Tbs. Coco Lopez Real Cream of Coconut

Combine, blend and pour.

MEXICAROLANS

1 part Carolans Irish Cream

1 part Jose Cuervo Tequila

Shake and serve over ice.

MEXICO MARTINI

1½ oz. Jose Cuervo Tequila

1 tbsp. Martini & Rossi
Extra Dry Vermouth

2-3 drops Vanilla Extract

Shake and strain into an iced
glass.

MEXICO ROSE

½ oz. Jose Cuervo Tequila

1 oz. Lime Juice

½ oz. Rose's Grenadine
(or DeKuyper
Crème de Cassis)

Combine in a rocks glass filled
with ice.

MIAMI SPECIAL

1 oz. Bacardi Light Rum

¼ oz. DeKuyper White
Crème de Menthe

¾ oz. Lemon or Rose's
Lime Juice

Blend.

MIDNIGHT MARTINI

1½ oz. Vox Vodka

½ oz. Chambord

Stir with ice and strain.
Garnish with a Lemon Twist.

*Gallery Lounge Sheraton
Seattle, Washington*

MILK & HONEY

Equal parts: Irish Mist,
Carolans Irish Cream. Served
in a rocks glass.

MIMOSA

3 oz. Champagne

2 oz. Orange Juice

Combine in a champagne
flute and stir.

MINT COOLER

1 oz. Bombay Sapphire
Gin

¼ oz. DeKuyper
Peppermint
Schnapps

Club Soda

In a tall glass with ice, combine the first two ingredients.
Fill the glass with Club Soda.

MINT JULEP

8 sprigs Mint

1 tsp. Superfine Sugar

2 tsp. Water

2½ oz. Knob Creek
Bourbon

In silver mug, muddle mint
leaves, superfine sugar, and
water. Fill glass or mug with
crushed ice and add Knob
Creek. Garnish with a mint
sprig.

MINTA

2 oz. Vox Vodka

fresh Crushed mint

1 tsp. Sugar

Shake and serve over crushed
ice.

MINTINI
OR
BOMBAY SAPPHIRE
GIN STINGER

2 parts Bombay Sapphire
Gin

1 part DeKuyper White
Crème de Menthe

Stir gently with ice and strain.

MIST OLD FASHIONED

1¼ oz. Irish Mist

Orange Slice

Cherry Bitters

Sugar

Club Soda or Water

Muddle the Orange, Cherry Bitters, and Sugar. Add Irish Mist. Top with Club Soda or Water.

MISTER MURPHY

1 part Irish Mist

1 part Bacardi Rum

1 part Orange juice

Serve in a rocks glass with a dash of Angostura bitters.

MISTER MURPHY II

1 part Irish Mist

1 part Bacardi Rum

1 part Orange Juice

dash Angostura Bitters

Combine in a rocks glass over ice with a dash of Angostura Bitters.

MISTIC BEACH

1¼ oz. Jose Cuervo Mistico

¾ oz. Cointreau

3 oz. Cranberry Juice

Combine over ice in a tall glass. Stir. Garnish with a Lemon Wedge.

MISTIC CHOCKLIC

¾ oz. Jose Cuervo Mistico

¾ oz. DeKuyper Coffee Liqueur

1 oz. Orange Juice

Shake and strain into a rocks glass with ice.

MISTIC MERLIN

¾ oz. Jose Cuervo Mistico

¾ oz. Cointreau

½ oz. Lime Juice

Shake with ice and strain.

MISTICO BANDITO

1 oz. Jose Cuervo Mistico

1 oz. Cranberry Juice

1 oz. Black Cherry Juice

Shake and serve in a shot glass.

MISTIC SHANDY

1¼ oz. Jose Cuervo Mistico

7 oz. Draft Beer

Combine Jose Cuervo Mistico and Beer in a glass.

MISTICO BERRY

1 oz. Jose Cuervo Mistico

1 oz. Cabernet Wine

splash Cointreau

splash Lime Juice

splash 7-Up

Sweet & Sour Mix

Combine first five ingredients in a tall glass with ice. Fill with Sweet & Sour Mix and garnish with a Lemon Wedge.

MISTICAL MAYAN

1¼ oz. Jose Cuervo Mistico

3 oz. Orange Juice

7-Up

Stir the first two ingredients with ice in a tall glass. Fill with 7-Up. Garnish with a Lime Wedge.

MISTICO CALIENTE

2 oz. Jose Cuervo Mistico

splash Tabasco Sauce

Combine in a shot glass and drop into a Draft Beer.

MISTICO CARIBBEAN SEA

1¼ oz. Jose Cuervo Mistico

¾ oz. DeKuyper Blue Curacao

½ oz. DeKuyper Peachtree Schnapps

Sweet & Sour Mix

Combine first three ingredients in a tall glass over ice. Fill with Sweet & Sour Mix.

MISTICO DESERT BERRY

1½ oz. Jose Cuervo Mistico

dash Chambord

Stir and strain into a shot glass.

MISTICO LEMONADE

1 oz. Jose Cuervo Mistico

1 oz. DeKuyper Orange Curacao

1 oz. Club Soda

1 oz. Cranberry Juice

Juice from ½ Lemon

Serve in a tall glass over ice.

MISTICO MARTINI

1 oz. Jose Cuervo Mistico

1 oz. Chambord

1 oz. Sweet & sour mix

Stir with ice and strain into a martini glass.

MISTICO MIRAGE

1½ oz. Jose Cuervo Mistico

1½ oz. Orange Juice

1½ oz. Tonic Water

Stir with ice and garnish with a Lime Wedge.

MISTICO MISSILE

1 oz. Jose Cuervo Mistico

½ oz. DeKuyper Peachtree Schnapps

splash Grapefruit Juice

Shake and strain. Serve in a shot glass.

MISTICO MORNING

1 oz. Jose Cuervo Mistico

1 oz. Pineapple Juice

1 oz. Orange Juice

splash Cointreau

Rose's Grenadine

Combine first four ingredients. Float Rose's Grenadine on top. Garnish with Lime.

MISTICO MYSTERY

1 oz. Jose Cuervo Mistico

1 oz. Cointreau

1 oz. Pineapple Juice

Shake and strain into a shot glass.

MISTICO SLIDE

½ oz. DeKuyper Coffee
Liqueur

½ oz. Carolans Irish
Cream

½ oz. Jose Cuervo Mistico

Layer ingredients in order listed, starting with DeKuyper
Coffee Liqueur in a shot glass.

MISTICO SPIKE

1½ oz. Jose Cuervo Mistico

3 oz. Ruby Red Grapefruit
Juice

dash Bitters

Stir with ice. Garnish with an
Orange Wedge.

MISTICO VERTIGO

1¼ oz. Jose Cuervo Mistico

2 oz. Sweet & Sour Mix

1 oz. Cranberry Juice

Juice from ½ Lemon

Stir with ice. Garnish with an
Orange Wheel.

MISTRAL

1 oz. Chambord

2 oz. Dry white wine

1 Tbs. Frozen strawberries
or raspberries

Mix in a blender with ice,
pour into a champagne glass.

MISTY MIST

1¼ oz. Irish Mist

Serve on shaved ice.

MOCHA MELT

1 oz.	Jose Cuervo Gold Tequila
5 oz.	Freshly Brewed Strong, Hot Coffee
1 pkg.	Hot Cocoa Mix (single-serving envelope)
½ oz.	DeKuyper Coffee Liqueur
	Whipped Cream

Combine ingredients in a glass and stir. Top with Whipped Cream.

MOCHA BERRY

2 oz.	Chambord
½ oz.	DeKuyper Dark Creme de Cacao
	Hot coffee
	Whipped cream

Serve in a coffee cup or mug.

MOCHA MINT

¾ oz.	Coffee-Flavored Brandy
¾ oz.	DeKuyper White Crème de Menthe
¾ oz.	DeKuyper White Crème de Cacao

Combine ingredients in a glass and stir. Strain into a cocktail glass.

MOCKING BIRD

1¼ oz.	Jose Cuervo Tequila
2 tsp.	DeKuyper White Crème de Menthe
1 oz.	Fresh Lime Juice

Shake and strain into a chilled cocktail glass with ice.

MODERN LOVE

½ oz. Orange juice

1½ oz. Grapefruit juice

1 oz. Bombay Sapphire Gin

1½ oz. Cointreau

Grapefruit peel spiral

Shake all ingredients with ice. Strain into a tumbler glass, over crushed ice. Stir.

MOJITO

2 oz. Bacardi Light Rum

8 Mint leaves

Juice of ½ lime

2 tsp. Sugar

Club Soda

In a Collins glass place mint leaves and lime, crush with a muddler or the back of a spoon, add sugar. Fill glass with ice, add Bacardi and top with club soda. Stir well and garnish with a sprig of mint.

Another one!

MONKEY GLAND

2 oz. Bombay Sapphire Gin

3 oz. Orange juice

¼ oz. Absinthe/Anis

shot Rose's Grenadine

Serve in a tall glass.

MOONLIGHT MARGARITA

1½ oz. Jose Cuervo Gold Tequila

1 oz. DeKuyper Blue Curacao

1 oz. Lime Juice

Rub the rim of a margarita glass with Lime Rind and dip it into Salt. Blend ingredients and serve in the prepared Salt glass. Garnish with a Lime Slice.

MOONRAKER

2 parts Jose Cuervo Especial

4 parts Pineapple Juice

1½ parts DeKuyper Blue
Curacao

Pour the Jose Cuervo Especial
and pineapple juice into a
rocks glass almost filled with
ice cubes. Stir well. Drop the
Curacao into the center of the
drink.

MORNING GLORY

¼ Pink grapefruit
chopped

1 passion fruit

2 Tsps. Fine sugar

¾ oz. Chambord

Ice

Champagne

Shake all but Champagne. Top
with Champagne.

MOONSHOT

1¼ oz. Bombay Sapphire
Gin

3 oz. Clam Juice

dash Red Pepper Sauce

Stir over ice cubes.

MOTHER PUCKER

1 oz. DeKuyper Sour
Apple Pucker

1 oz. DeKuyper
Cheri-Beri Pucker

1 oz. DeKuyper Grape
Pucker

splash Orange juice

squeeze Lime

1 Maraschino cherry

Shake, serve in a tall glass with
ice.

MOUNT GRINDER

1½ oz. Bacardi Rum

2 oz. Cranberry Juice

splash 7-Up

Combine in a tall glass.

MOUNTAIN MELTER

1 oz. Jose Cuervo Gold
Tequila

½ oz. Cointreau

5 oz. Hot Water

1 pkg. Hot Cocoa Mix
(single-serving envelope)

Combine ingredients in a
glass and stir. Top with
Whipped Cream and Ground
Cinnamon.

MS. TEA

1¼ oz. Irish Mist

3 oz. Iced Tea

Mix with ice; serve over ice.

MUDSLIDE

¼ oz. DeKuyper Coffee
Liqueur

1 oz. Vox Vodka

¼ oz. Carolans Irish
Cream

Cola

Combine first three ingredients in a glass with ice and fill with Cola.

MUDSLIDE II

¾ oz. DeKuyper Coffee
Liqueur

¾ oz. Carolans Irish
Cream

Pour over ice in a rocks glass.

MURPHY'S DREAM

1 part Irish Mist

1 part Bombay Sapphire
Gin

1 part Lemon juice

Sugar

Shake. Serve straight up or on
the rocks.

MURPH'S DREAM

1 part Irish Mist

1 part Vox Vodka

1 part Lemon Juice

Sugar

Shake. Serve straight up or
over ice.

NAKED MARTINI

2 oz. Vox Vodka or
Bombay Sapphire
Gin

Serve over ice.

NARRAGANSETT

1½ oz. Knob Creek
Bourbon

½ oz. Martini & Rossi
Rosso Vermouth

3 dashes DeKuyper Anisette

Stir in old-fashioned glass
with ice cubes. Add a twist of
lemon peel.

NATION COCKTAIL

1½ oz. Jose Cuervo Gold
Tequila

1½ oz. Pineapple Juice

1½ oz. Orange Juice

¼ oz. DeKuyper Blue
Curacao

Combine first three ingredients over ice. Float Blue
Curacao. You can also serve
this one without ice.

NEGRONI

1 part Campari

1 part Vox Vodka

1 part Martini & Rossi
        Rosso Vermouth

Shake and serve on the rocks
or straight up.

NELLIE
JANE

1¼ oz. Irish Mist

¼ oz. DeKuyper Peachtree
        Schnapps

3 oz. Orange juice

1 oz. Ginger Ale

Mix all but Ginger Ale. Float
Ginger Ale.

NERVOUS
BREAKDOWN

1½ oz. Vox Vodka

½ oz. Chambord

splash Cranberry Juice

        Soda

Combine the first three ingredients in a tall glass. Fill with
Soda.

NEW
YORKER

1 oz. Knob Creek
       Bourbon

2 oz. Cranberry juice

2 oz. Grapefruit juice

½ oz. Rose's Lime Juice

¼ oz. Rose's Grenadine

Stir ingredients together and
serve over ice in a wine glass.

NEWTON'S COCKTAIL

1¼ oz. DeKuyper Sour
        Apple Pucker

¾ oz. DeKuyper Melon
       Liqueur

3 oz. Sweet & sour mix

NIGHT AND DAY

½ part Jose Cuervo Especial

½ part DeKuyper Coffee
       Liqueur

½ part Cola

Pour all the ingredients into a
shot glass.

NUT 'N' HOLLI

1 part Irish Mist

1 part Disaronno Amaretto

1 part Carolans Irish
       Cream

Shake. Serve straight up in a
shot glass.

NUTS & BERRYS

½ oz. Vox Vodka

½ oz. Disaronno Amaretto

½ oz. DeKuyper Coffee
       Liqueur

¼ oz. Cream

Combine with ice and shake.
Strain and serve straight up in
a rocks glass.

NUTS AND CHERRYS

1 oz. DeKuyper Cheri-Beri Pucker

½ oz. Disaronno Amaretto

Shake with ice, strain into shot glass.

N.Y. COSMO

1½ oz. Vox Vodka

½ oz. Chambord

1 oz. Sweet and sour mix

2 oz. Cranberry juice

dash Orange juice

Ice

Shake and pour over ice in a cocktail glass.

O & CRANBERRY

1½ oz. Bacardi O™

5 oz. Cranberry Juice

Orange Wedge garnish

Stir in a tall glass over ice.

O & CREAM

1½ oz. Bacardi O™

1½ oz. Carolans Irish Cream

Shake with ice. Serve in a shooter glass or a rocks glass over ice.

O & TONIC

1½ oz. Bacardi O™

6 oz. Tonic Water

Orange Twist garnish

In a tall glass with ice.

O BIG DADDY
(FROM TU TU TANGO)

½ oz. Bacardi O™

½ oz. Bacardi Razz

¼ oz. Pineapple juice

¼ oz. Cranberry juice

Combine all into shaker,
strain into martini glass, sink
grenadine garnish with orange
twist.

O CIRCLE MARTINI

1½ oz. Bacardi O™

½ oz. Bombay Sapphire
Gin

splash Cream

Shake with ice; strain and
serve in chilled martini glass;
garnish with an orange twist.

O COSMOPOLITAN

2 oz. Bacardi O™

1 oz. Cointreau

½ oz. Lime Juice

splash Cranberry Juice

Orange Wedge
garnish

Serve on the rocks with
orange wedge.

O LOOK MARTINI COCKTAIL

2 oz. Bacardi O™

½ oz. Pink Grapefruit
Juice

½ oz. Cointreau

½ oz. Sweet & Sour Mix

splash Lemon/Lime Soda

Serve up in a sugar-rimmed
glass; garnish with a grapefruit slice.

O MADRAS

1½ oz. Bacardi O™

4 oz. Cranberry Juice

1 oz. Orange Juice

Blend with ice; serve in a tall glass garnished with Maraschino cherry and orange slice.

O MY MARTINI COCKTAIL

2 oz. Bacardi O™

1 oz. DeKuyper Blue Curacao

splash Sweet & Sour Mix

Shake with ice; strain into a chilled martini glass. Top with grenadine.

O.J. MIST

2 oz. Irish Mist

3 oz. Orange Juice

Combine in a tall glass over ice.

OATMEAL COOKIE

Equal parts:

Carolans Irish Cream

Goldschlager

Butterscotch Schnapps

Shake and serve as a shot.

O-CHERI BABY

1¼ oz. DeKuyper Cheri-Beri Pucker chilled

¼ oz. Vox Vodka

Serve as a shot.

OLD FASHIONED

1½ oz. American or Canadian Whisky

¼ tsp. Superfine Sugar

2 dashes Angostura Bitters

splash of Club Soda

Cherry and Orange Slice

Muddle the Cherry (without stem), Orange Slice, Sugar, and a splash of Club Soda. Add the remaining ingredients and stir.

OLD LAY

¾ oz. Cointreau

1¼ oz. Jose Cuervo Tequila

1 dash Rose's Grenadine

¾ oz. Lime Juice

Shake with ice and strain.

OLYMPIC

1 oz. Hennessy Cognac

1 oz. Cointreau

1 oz. Orange juice

Shake and pour into a chilled cocktail glass.

OOH, LA LA MARTINI COCKTAIL

1 oz. Bacardi O™

1 oz. Orange Juice

splash Cointreau

Shake with ice; strain and serve in chilled martini glass garnished with orange slice.

ORANGE BLOSSOM

1¼ oz. Vox Vodka

3 oz. Orange juice

1 tsp. Superfine sugar

Stir with ice in a tall glass.

ORANGE BLOSSOM II

1¼ oz. Vox Vodka

½ oz. Cointreau

3 oz. Orange juice

1 tsp. Superfine sugar

Stir with ice in a tall glass.

ORANGE BLOSSOM III

¼ oz. Bombay Sapphire Gin

1 oz. Sweetened Lemon Mix

2 oz. Orange Juice

Shake with ice and pour on the rocks.

ORANGE CRUSH

½ oz. Cointreau

1 oz. Vox Vodka

½ oz. Orange Juice

dash 7-Up

Shake with ice and strain. Top with 7-Up.

ORANGE CUERVO RICKEY

2 parts Jose Cuervo Especial

2 Tbs. Cointreau

½ Lime

Chilled Club Soda or Seltzer

In a tall highball glass filled with ice cubes, combine Jose Cuervo Especial and Cointreau. Squeeze the lime over the drink and drop the lime into the glass. Top off with club soda.

ORANGE MARGARITA

1½ oz. Jose Cuervo Gold Tequila

½ oz. Cointreau

3 oz. Orange Juice

½ oz. Sweet & Sour Mix

Blend. Garnish with Strawberries.

ORANGE RUSH

1 oz. Bacardi O™

½ oz. DeKuyper Peachtree
Schnapps

2 oz. Orange Juice

1 oz. Pineapple Juice

1 oz. Cranberry Juice

Blend with ice; serve in tall
glass garnished with an
orange slice.

ORANGE SUNSET

1 oz. Bombay Sapphire
Gin

¼ oz. DeKuyper Creme
de Banana Liqueur

1 oz. Sweetened Lemon
Mix

1 oz. Orange Juice

Shake well with ice and serve
on the rocks.

ORANGE WHIP

1 oz. Bacardi O™

¾ oz. Bombay Sapphire
Gin

2 oz. Orange Juice

1 oz. Sweet & Sour Mix

Shake with ice; serve in tall
glass with ice and top with
grenadine.

ORANGESICLE

1½ oz. Bacardi O™

1½ oz. Cream

½ oz. Orange Juice

Blend. Serve in a powdered
sugar rimmed glass; garnish
with orange wheel.

ORANGETINI

1½ oz. Vox Vodka

dash Martini & Rossi
Extra Dry Vermouth

splash Cointreau

Stir gently and strain over ice.
Garnish with an Orange Peel.

ORGASM

1 part Carolans Irish
Cream

1 part Disaronno Amaretto

1 part DeKuyper Coffee
Liqueur

Shake with ice and strain into
shot glass.

ORGASM II

1 part Disaronno Amaretto

1 part DeKuyper Coffee
Liqueur

1 part Carolans Irish
Cream

1 part Cream

Shake with ice and strain into
a shot glass.

ORIENT EXPRESS

1 oz. Pineapple juice

1 oz. Grapefruit juice

1 oz. Bacardi Light Rum

1 oz. Cointreau

Rose's Grenadine

Shake pineapple juice, grapefruit juice, Bacardi and
Cointreau with ice. Strain
into a tumbler glass with ice.
Add a drop of grenadine. Stir.
Garnish pineapple slice and
mint leaves.

OTB

2 oz. Bacardi O™

2 oz. Iced Tea

Serve over crushed ice with splash of soda; garnish with an orange twist.

O™ MARTINI COCKTAIL

2 oz. Bacardi O™

¼ oz. Martini & Rossi Extra Dry Vermouth

Orange Twist garnish

In a rocks glass over ice or straight up in a martini glass.

OUTRIGGER

1 oz. Vox Vodka

½ oz. DeKuyper Peachtree Schnapps

1 dash Lime Juice

2 oz. Pineapple Juice

Combine with ice in a shaker and shake. Strain over ice into a rocks glass.

OYSTER SHOOTER

1 oz. Vox Vodka

1 Raw Oyster

1 tsp. Cocktail Sauce

Pour Vox Vodka over the Oyster and Sauce in a small rocks glass and stir. Add a squeeze of Lemon. You can also add a dash of horseradish.

PADDY COCKTAIL

1½ oz. Tullamore Dew
        Irish Whiskey

¾ oz.   Martini & Rossi
        Rosso Vermouth

Several dashes Angostura
bitters. Stir.

PADDY O'ROCCO

1½ oz. Irish Mist

3 oz.   Orange Juice

splash Disaronno Amaretto

Mix Irish Mist and Orange
Juice. Top with a splash of
Disaronno Amaretto.

PAISLEY

2 oz.   Bombay Sapphire
        Gin

½ oz.   Dewar's Scotch

½ oz.   Martini & Rossi Dry
        Vermouth

Garnish with a twist as you
stir.

PALOMA
(DOVE)

2 parts Jose Cuervo Especial

         Squirt®

         Lime Wedge

         Salt

Rub the rim of a chilled tall
highball glass with lime and
dip it into the salt to coat. Put
ice into the glass; add Jose
Cuervo Especial. Add some
more salt if you'd like and fill
the glass with the Squirt.
Garnish with lime.

PANZER

1 part Vox Vodka

1 part Bombay Sapphire
        Gin

1 part Cointreau

Combine in shaker with ice.
Strain into chilled cocktail
glass.

PEACH BANANA DAIQUIRI

1½ oz.   Bacardi Light Rum

½ Med.   Banana, diced

1 oz.   Fresh Lime Juice

¼ cup   Sliced Peaches
         (fresh, frozen, or
         canned)

Blend.

PEACH BLOSSOM

1 oz.   DeKuyper Peachtree
         Schnapps

½ oz.   Disaronno Amaretto

1 scp   Vanilla Ice Cream

Blend.

PEACH COBBLER

1¼ oz.   DeKuyper Peachtree
         Schnapps

5 oz.   Hot Apple
         Cider

Serve in mug. Top with cream.

PEACH CREAMY

¾ oz.   DeKuyper Peachtree
         Schnapps

½ oz.   DeKuyper White
         Creme de Cacao

2 oz.   Cream

Shake well with ice and strain into cocktail glass.

PEACH IRISH

1½ oz. Tullamore Dew Irish Whiskey

1 Ripe Peach (peeled, pitted, and sliced)

½ cup Fresh Lime Juice

1 oz. DeKuyper Apricot Brandy

1 Tbsp. Superfine Sugar

dash Vanilla Extract

Blend.

PEACH MARGARITA

1½ oz. Jose Cuervo Gold Tequila

1 oz. Cointreau

1 oz. Lime Juice

½ cup Peaches (canned)

Blend. Garnish with Peach Slices.

PEACH ON THE BEACH

¾ oz. DeKuyper Peachtree Schnapps

½ oz. Vox Vodka

2 oz. Orange Juice

2 oz. Cranberry Juice

Build over cubed ice in a tall glass.

PHEOBE SNOW

1½ oz. Hennessy Cognac

1½ oz. Dubonnet Red

dash Pernod

Shake and pour into a chilled cocktail glass.

219

PICNIC PUNCH

Makes 5-6 servings

6½ oz. Jose Cuervo Tequila

3½ oz. Chambord

10 oz. Fruit Puree

3½ oz. Mango Nectar

7 oz. Fruit Tea, steeped, sweetened and chilled

1 lime

Mix in a large punch bowl.

PIÑA COLADA

2 oz. Bacardi Light Rum

6 oz. Pineapple Juice

2 oz. Coco Lopez Cream of Coconut

Blend with ice, garnish with a pineapple spear.

PINEAPPLE BOMB

1 part Bacardi Light Rum

1 part Bacardi Dark Rum

1 part Pineapple Juice

Shake with ice and strain into a shot glass.

PINEAPPLE-ORANGE MARGARITA

1½ parts Jose Cuervo Especial

3 parts Jose Cuervo Margarita Mix

1 part Pineapple Juice

1 Tbs. Simple Syrup

Pineapple Spears

Maraschino Cherries

Combine pineapple juice, Jose Cuervo Especial, Jose Cuervo Margarita Mix and simple syrup in large mixing glass. Add ice cubes and stir to blend well. Strain the contents into a margarita glass. Garnish with pineapple spears and Maraschino cherries.

PINEAPPLE TWIST

1½ oz. Bacardi Rum

6 oz. Pineapple Juice

splash Lemon Juice

Shake and pour into a tall glass over ice.

PINK BANANA

2 oz. DeKuyper Creme de Banana

2 oz. Pink lemonade

Shake and serve in a tall glass.

PINK CADDY

1½ parts Jose Cuervo Tequila

1½ parts Cranberry juice

½ part Freshly squeezed lime juice

¾ parts Cointreau

Shake first three ingredients with ice and strain into martini glass. Serve Cointreau in a shot glass as an accompaniment to be poured into the cocktail between sips.

PINK CADILLAC WITH HAWAIIAN PLATES

1¼ oz. Jose Cuervo 1800 Tequila

2 oz. Pineapple Juice

2 oz. Cranberry Juice

½ oz. Sweet & Sour Mix

Combine in a rocks glass. Garnish with a Lime Wedge.

PINK CREAM FIZZ

2 oz. Bombay Sapphire Gin

Lemon juice

Sugar

Light cream

Rose's Grenadine

Club soda

Top with club soda.

PINK ELEPHANT

splash Rose's Grenadine

2 oz. Bombay Sapphire Gin

Shake and serve over ice.

PINK ELEPHANT EARS

2 oz. Vox Vodka

2 oz. Pink lemonade

½ Lime, freshly squeezed

Shake and serve over ice.

PINK FIX

2 oz. Bombay Sapphire Gin

2 oz. Lemon juice

splash Rose's Grenadine

Shake and serve on the rocks or as a shot.

PINK FLAMINGO

1 oz. DeKuyper Wilderberry Schnapps

2 oz. Cranberry juice

shot Sweet & sour mix

Pour together over ice and stir.

PINK GIN & TONIC

2 oz. Bombay Sapphire Gin

Tonic Water

½ oz. Campari

Lime slice

Serve in a tall glass.

PINK GIN

2 oz. Bombay Sapphire Gin

splash Angostura Bitters

Serve over ice.

PINK HEART

½ oz. DeKuyper Creme de Cacao

½ oz. Chambord

Milk or cream

Ice

In rocks glass filled with ice add Creme de Cacao and Chambord. Fill with cream or milk. Stir.

PINK HOUND

1 part Vox Vodka

1 part Bombay Sapphire Gin

3 parts Pink grapefruit juice

Shake ingredients with ice and strain into glass.

PINK LADY

3 oz. Bombay Sapphire Gin

5 dashes Rose's Grenadine

2 oz. Half and Half or Vanilla Ice Cream

Shake or Blend, garnish with Maraschino cherry.

PINK LEMONADE

2 oz. Vox Vodka

1 oz. Sour mix

1 oz. Cranberry juice

½ oz. Lime juice

Shake and serve in a tall glass.

PINK LEMONADE II

1¼ oz. Vox Vodka

1 oz. Cranberry Juice

1¼ oz. Sweet & Sour Mix

½ tsp. Sugar

Club Soda

Combine Vox Vodka, Sugar, Sweet & Sour Mix, and Cranberry Juice in a tall glass. Stir to dissolve Sugar. Add ice and top with Club Soda. Add a squeeze of Lime.

PINK LIMÓN

2 oz. Bacardi Limón

1 oz. Sweet & Sour Mix

2 oz. Cranberry juice

½ oz. Rose's Grenadine

2 oz. Cream or Half & Half

Shake or blend.

PINK PANTHER

1½ oz. Jose Cuervo Tequila

¾ oz. Lemon Juice

¾ oz. Cream

½ oz. Rose's Grenadine

Blend with crushed ice and strain into a chilled glass.

PINK PANTHER II

1¼ oz. Bacardi Light Rum

¾ oz. Lemon Juice

¾ oz. Cream

½ oz. Rose's Grenadine

Blend with crushed ice and strain.

PINK PANTHER III

2½ oz. Bacardi Còco

1 oz. Vox Vodka

½ oz. DeKuyper Peachtree Schnapps

½ oz. Cointreau

splash Grapefruit

splash Orange juice

dash Rose's Grenadine

Shake and strain ingredients into a chilled 10 oz. martini glass. Sink a splash of grenadine syrup and garnish with an orange wheel.

PINK PILLOW

2 oz. Vox Vodka

splash Rose's Grenadine

2 oz. Sweet & Sour mix

Shake with Ice. Serve in tall glass.

PINK PITCH

2 oz. Vox Vodka

½ oz. Licor 43

½ oz. Milk

splash Rose's Grenadine

Shake with ice and serve on the rocks.

PINK PONY

2 parts Jose Cuervo Especial

⅓ cup Chilled Cranberry Juice

¼ cup Chilled Apple Juice

Chilled Club Soda or Seltzer Water

In a rocks glass filled with ice cubes, combine the Jose Cuervo Especial, the cranberry juice and the apple juice. Top off the drink with the club soda.

PINK PUSSYCAT

1½ oz. Bombay Sapphire
Gin

¼ oz. Chambord

2¼ oz. Pineapple juice

splash Rose's Grenadine

Shake and serve over ice.

PINK PUSSYCAT II

1½ oz. Vox Vodka

½ oz. Pineapple juice

splash Rose's Grenadine

Pour over ice into highball
glass. Garnish with sliced
strawberry.

PINK RANGER

1 oz. Vox Vodka

½ oz. Coco Lopez Real
Cream of Coconut

1 oz. DeKuyper Peachtree
Schnapps

1 oz. Cranberry juice

1 oz. Pineapple juice

Blend and serve in a tall glass.

PINK ROSE

2 oz. Vox Vodka

½ oz. DeKuyper Peachtree
Schnapps

dash Cranberry juice

Shake and serve on the rocks.

PINK RUSSIAN

1 oz. Tequila Rose

½ oz. DeKuyper Coffee
Liqueur

½ oz. Vox Vodka

½ oz. Milk

Shake and serve on the rocks.

PINK SIN MARTINI

¾ part DeKuyper
Cinnamon
Schnapps

1 part DeKuyper White
Creme de Cacao

1½ parts Vox Vodka

1 part Cranberry juice

Shake and strain into glass.

PINK SQUIRREL

1 oz. Creme de Noyeaux

1 oz. DeKuyper Creme de Cacao

2 oz. Light cream

Shake and serve up in a martini glass.

PIXIE STICK

2 oz. DeKuyper Cheri-Beri Pucker

2 oz. Sweet and Sour Mix

splash 7-Up

Serve as a mixed drink.

POISON APPLE

$\frac{1}{4}$ oz. Knob Creek Bourbon

$\frac{1}{4}$ oz. DeKuyper Sour Apple Pucker

$\frac{1}{4}$ oz. Vox Vodka

$\frac{1}{4}$ oz. Bacardi Rum

$\frac{1}{4}$ oz. DeKuyper Creme de Banana

1 oz. Sweet & sour mix

Shake and serve in a tall glass.

POISON APPLE II

$1\frac{1}{4}$ parts DeKuyper Sour Apple Pucker

$\frac{3}{4}$ part DeKuyper Thrilla Vanilla Liqueur

1 part Rose's Grenadine

Pour over ice in tall glass. Fill with lemon-lime soda.

POISON RED APPLE

½ oz.   Knob Creek
        Bourbon

½ oz.   DeKuyper Sour
        Apple Pucker

½ oz.   Vox Vodka

½ oz.   Bacardi Rum

½ oz.   DeKuyper Creme de
        Banana

2 oz.   Sweet & sour mix

Shake with ice and pour in tall
glass. Top with cranberry
juice.

POLO

1¼ oz.   Bombay Sapphire
         Gin

2 oz.   Grapefruit Juice

2 oz.   Orange Juice

In a tall glass with ice, fill with
half grapefruit juice and half
orange juice.

POUSSE-CAFÈ STANDISH

½ oz.   Rose's Grenadine

½ oz.   DeKuyper White
        Crème de Menthe

½ oz.   Galliano

½ oz.   Kummel

½ oz.   Hennessy Cognac

Layer this drink in the order
listed. Start with Rose's
Grenadine on the bottom and
finish with Hennessy Cognac
on top.

PRAIRIE FIRE

1½ oz.   Jose Cuervo
         Tequila

2 or 3 drops Tabasco

Combine in a shot glass.

PRESBYTERIAN

2 oz. Knob Creek
Bourbon

Ginger Ale

Club Soda

Pour the Knob Creek
Bourbon into a chilled highball glass. Add ice cubes. Top
off the glass with equal parts
of Ginger Ale and Soda.

PRESIDENTE

$\frac{1}{4}$ oz. Martini & Rossi Dry
Vermouth

$\frac{3}{4}$ oz. Martini & Rossi
Rosso Vermouth

1$\frac{1}{2}$ oz. Bacardi Light Rum

1 splash Rose's Grenadine

Mix with ice and serve.

PRINCE EDWARD

$\frac{1}{2}$ oz. Drambuie

1 oz. Dewar's Scotch

$\frac{1}{2}$ oz. Lillet Blanc

Orange Slice

Combine all ingredients,
except orange slice, with
cracked ice in a cocktail shaker. Shake well and pour into
chilled old-fashioned glass.
Garnish with orange slice.

PROPAGANDA

5 strawberries
chopped

2 Tsps. Fine sugar

$\frac{3}{4}$ oz. Sugar syrup

Ice

1 oz. Vox Vodka

1 oz. Chambord

Shake. Serve on rocks.

PRIVILEGE & GINGER

1 oz. Hennessy
       Privilege

Over ice in a snifter, fill with
gingerale.

PUCKER APPLE-ADE

1 shot DeKuyper Sour
        Apple Pucker

Fill with lemonade. Serve on
rocks in tall glass.

PUCKER CHERI-ADE

1 shot DeKuyper Cheri-
        Beri Pucker

Fill with lemonade; serve on
the rocks in tall glass.

PUCKER PANDEMONIUM FREEZE

2 oz. DeKuyper Sour
       Apple Pucker

1 oz. Vanilla ice cream

Blend.

PUCKER PANDEMONIUM FREEZE II

2 oz. DeKuyper
       Cheri-Beri Pucker

1 oz. Vanilla Ice cream

Blend.

PUCKER UP

1 oz. DeKuyper Sour
      Apple Pucker

Fill glass with lemon-lime
soda and ice.

PUCKERED UP RUSSIAN

2 parts DeKuyper Sour
        Apple Pucker

1 part Vox Vodka (frozen)

Combine, serve as shot.

PUCKERED DISASTER

Equal parts:

1 oz. Avalanche Blue

½ oz. After Shock Liqueur

1 oz. DeKuyper Sour Apple
      Pucker

Shake with ice.

PUCKERITA

½ oz. DeKuyper Cheri-
      Beri Pucker

1 oz. Jose Cuervo Tequila

      Sweet & Sour Mix

dash Lime juice

Shake with ice, serve in a tall
glass.

PUCKERED MADRAS

1 oz. DeKuyper Sour Apple
      Pucker

1 oz. Vox Vodka

1 oz. Cranberry juice

1 oz. Orange juice

Shake with ice.

PULCO

2 oz. Jose Cuervo 1800
      Tequila

½ oz. Cointreau

1½ oz. Lime Juice

Combine over ice.

PUNCH IN THE PANTS

1 oz. Bacardi O™

1 oz. Bacardi Limón

splash Cointreau

splash Sweet & Sour Mix

3 oz. Orange Soda

Blend with ice.

PURPLE HAZE

1 oz. Chambord

1 oz. Vox Vodka

1 oz. Cranberry Juice or Sour Mix

Combine in a shot glass.

PURPLE HAZE MARTINI COCKTAIL

2 oz. Bacardi O™

2 oz. Lemonade

¼ oz. Rose's Grenadine

½ oz. DeKuyper Blue Curacao

Shake with ice; strain and serve in a chilled martini glass; garnish with an orange slice.

PURPLE HOOTER

½ oz. Vox Vodka

½ oz. Chambord

½ oz. Cranberry Juice

splash Club Soda

Shake and strain Vox Vodka, Chambord and Cranberry Juice. Top with a splash of Club Soda.

PURPLE ORCHID

1 part DeKuyper White
        Crème de Cacao

1 part DeKuyper
        Blackberry Brandy

1 part Cream

Combine in a shot glass.

PURPLE PASSION

1¼ oz. Vox Vodka

2 oz.   Grapefruit Juice

2 oz.   Grape Juice

Combine ingredients and stir.
Serve in a collins glass.

QUEEN ELIZABETH MARTINI

1½ oz. Bombay Sapphire
        Gin

splash Martini & Rossi
        Extra Dry Vermouth

splash Benedictine

Stir in cocktail glass. Strain
and serve up or on the rocks.
Add lemon twist or olives.

RACER'S EDGE

1½ oz. Bacardi Light Rum

¼ oz.   DeKuyper Green
        Crème de Menthe

        Grapefruit Juice

Pour Bacardi into a glass half
filled with ice. Fill with
Grapefruit Juice and float
Crème de Menthe.

RAIN DROP

2 oz. Vox Vodka

1 oz. Lemon Juice

Sugar

Shake. Serve in a sugar-coated chilled cocktail glass with a squeeze of Lemon.

RAMOS FIZZ

1½ oz. Bombay Sapphire Gin

1 tbsp. Powdered Sugar

3-4 drops Orange-Flower Water

Juice ½ Lime

Juice ½ Lemon

1 Egg White

1½ oz. Cream

Seltzer

2 drops Vanilla Extract

Mix ingredients in the order given. Add crushed ice. Shake. Strain into a tall glass.

RASMOPOLITAN

1¼ parts VOX Raspberry Vodka

½ part Cointreau

1 part Cranberry juice

squeeze Fresh lime juice

Mix in shaker half-filled with ice. Pour into a chilled martini glass. Garnish with fresh raspberries or a lime peel.

RASPBERRY BREEZE

1 part VOX Raspberry Vodka

2 parts Cranberry juice

2 parts Grapefruit juice

Shake all ingredients with ice and pour into martini glass.

RASPBERRY DELIGHT

¾ oz. Drambuie

¾ oz. Chambord

½ oz. DeKuyper Coffee
Liqueur

Fresh Raspberries

1 scoop Ice Cream

Blend.

RASPBERRY FLIRTINI

1 part VOX Raspberry
Vodka

½ part Chambord

1 part Champagne (float)

Mix VOX Raspberry and
Chambord in shaker half
filled with ice. Pour into a
champagne flute and top with
Champagne. Garnish with
fresh raspberries.

RASPBERRY HONEY NUTS

1 oz. Honey Walnut
Cream Liqueur

1 oz. Chambord

2 oz. Half and Half

5 Raspberries

Shake and serve in a rocks
glass. Top with raspberries.

RASPBERRY KIR

1 oz. VOX Raspberry
Vodka

¼ oz. Champagne

In a chilled fluted champagne
glass, garnish with Raspberry.

RASPBERRY MARGARITA

2½ oz. Bacardi Razz

1 oz. Cointreau

½ oz. Rose's Lime Juice

1 oz. Sour mix

splash Cranberry juice

Pour over ice into a rocks glass. Garnish with a lime.

Matthew "Woody" Woodburn
Sinibar
Chicago, IL

RASPBERRY MARTINI

2 parts VOX Raspberry Vodka

¼ part Chambord

6 fresh Raspberries

Muddle raspberries with VOX Raspberry Vodka and Chambord. Shake with ice and strain into glass.

RASPBERRY MINT DAIQUIRI

1½ oz. Bacardi Light Rum

½ oz. Cranberry juice

2 oz. Sweet and sour mix

1 oz. Raspberry Mint Puree

½ oz. Chambord

Shake or blend, serve in a tall glass.

RASPBERRY SPRITZER

1¼ parts VOX Raspberry Vodka

¾ part Chambord

3 parts Lemon lime soda

Combine VOX Raspberry Vodka and lemon lime soda in a tall glass filled with ice. Add Chambord, letting it gently sink to the bottom. Garnish with a fresh raspberry.

RASPBERRY TRUFFLE

1½ parts VOX Raspberry
Vodka

1 part DeKuyper White
Creme de Cacao

½ part Chambord

¾ part Half & half

Mix in a shaker half-filled
with ice. Pour into a martini
glass rimmed with cocoa.

RAZZ-MA-TAZZ

1½ oz. Vox Vodka

½ oz. Chambord

1½ oz. Club Soda

Serve over ice in a tall glass,
chilled.

RAZZ LEMONADE

16 oz. glass mug filled with
ice cubes

8 oz. Minute Maid
Lemonade

1 oz. Monin Raspberry
Syrup

1¼ oz. Bacardi Razz Rum

Fill glass with ice. Add ingredients in order of listing. Stir
well to blend. Serve with
lemon wedge.

RED HEADED MEXICAN

1¼ oz. Jose Cuervo Clásico

4 oz. Lemon-lime soda
(Sprite/7-Up)

¼ oz. Cranberry juice

Serve in a tall glass.

RED HOT MAMA

1¼ oz. Bacardi Rum

4 oz. Cranberry Juice

2 oz. Club Soda

Combine over ice.

RED RAIDER

1 oz. Knob Creek
Bourbon

½ oz. Cointreau

1 oz. Lemon Juice

1 dash Grenadine

Shake with ice and strain into
a tall glass.

RED REBEL

1 part Jose Cuervo Clásico

4 parts Lemon-Lime Soda

splash Cranberry Juice

Combine tequila and lemon-
lime soda in a rocks glass with
ice. Stir. Add splash of cranberry juice. Garnish with
lemon or orange peel.

ROAD KILL

1 part Tullamore Dew Irish
Whiskey

1 part Knob Creek
Bourbon

1 part Bacardi Rum
(151-proof)

Combine in a shot glass.

ROB ROY

2 oz. Dewar's White Label

dash Martini & Rossi
Rosso or Dry
Vermouth

Stir over ice and strain. You
can also serve over ice.

ROOTY-TOOTY

1¼ oz. DeKuyper Old
Tavern Root
Beer Schnapps

3 oz. Orange Juice

Mix with ice in a blender,
serve over ice in an on-the-
rocks glass.

ROYAL BOMBAY SAPPHIRE GIN FIZZ

2 oz. Bombay Sapphire Gin

½ oz. Cointreau

1 oz. Sweet & Sour Mix

1 oz. Club Soda

Fill mixing glass with ice and all ingredients except club soda. Shake and strain into chilled glass. Fill with club soda.

RUBY SLIPPER MARTINI

2 oz. Bombay Sapphire Gin

¼ oz. Cointreau

1-2 splashes Rose's Grenadine

1 dash DeKuyper Peppermint Schnapps

Garnish with a mint leaf (Set it on the edge of the drink and let it stick out.)

RUDE COSMOPOLITAN

1 part Jose Cuervo Clásico

¼ part Cointreau

1 part Cranberry Juice

Juice from a Whole Lime

Shake all ingredients with ice. Strain into a chilled cocktail glass. Garnish with orange peel.

RUE L'ORANGE MARTINI COCKTAIL

1½ oz. Bacardi O™

1 oz. Lillet Blanc

1¼ oz. Cranberry Juice

splash Sweet & Sour Mix

Shake; strain and serve in a chilled martini glass; garnish with an orange twist.

RUM & COKE

1½ oz. Bacardi Light Rum

3 oz. Cola

Stir ingredients with ice.

RUSTY NAIL

½ oz. Drambuie

1½ oz. Dewar's Scotch

Serve on the rocks.

S.O.S.

3 parts Bacardi O™

1 part Chambord

2 parts Sweet & sour

1 part Cranberry juice

Shake all ingredients with ice and strain into shot glass.

SA PUCKER SUCKER

½ oz. DeKuyper Sour Apple Pucker

½ oz. DeKuyper Coffee Liqueur

½ oz. Orange juice

Combine, serve as shot.

SAKE O MARTINI COCKTAIL

2 oz. Bacardi O™

¼ oz. Sake

¼ oz. Cranberry Juice

Shake with ice; strain into a chilled martini glass.

SALT LICK

1¼ oz. Vox Vodka

2 oz. Bitter Lemon Soda

2 oz. Grapefruit Juice

Pour over ice in salt-rimmed wine glass.

SALTY DOG

1¼ oz. Bombay Sapphire
        Gin

        Grapefruit Juice

        Salt

Wet rim of tall glass with juice or water and dip into salt to coat (optional). Pour Bombay over ice; fill with grapefruit juice and stir.

SANTA FE MAGGIE

1¼ oz. Jose Cuervo Gold
        Tequila

½ oz.   Cointreau

2 oz.   Sweet & Sour Mix

2 oz.   Cranberry Juice

Combine ingredients over ice and garnish with a Lime Wedge.

SAPLING

1 oz. Laird's Applejack

1 oz. Cointreau

1 oz. Lime Juice

Shake well with ice; strain into tall glass filled with shaved ice. Garnish with sprig of mint.

SAPPHIRE & TONIC

2 oz. Bombay Sapphire

       Tonic

squeeze Lime

In a tall glass filled with ice, add Bombay Sapphire and fill with tonic. Add a squeeze of lime.

SAPPHIRE MARTINI

2 oz. Bombay Sapphire
Gin

½ oz. Martini & Rossi
Dry Vermouth

Garnish with an olive.

SAPPHIRE ROSE

2 oz. Bombay Sapphire
Gin

fresh Grapefruit juice

Sugar syrup

Maraschino liqueur

Combine in a tall glass.

SAPPHIRE SOUR

2 oz. Bombay Sapphire
Gin

juice of ½ Lemon

½ tsp. Powdered Sugar

Mix ingredients with cracked
ice in shaker; strain into martini glass.

SATIN ROUGE
MARTINI COCKTAIL

1¼ oz. Bacardi O™

½ oz. Tropico Liqueur

¼ oz. Cherry Juice

½ oz. Pineapple Juice

Serve in chilled glass; garnish
with lemon twist.

SCARLETT KISS

Mix Drambuie with cranberry
juice and serve over ice in a
tall glass.

SCARLETT O'HARA

1½ oz. Southern Comfort

3 oz. Cranberry Juice

Combine with ice and stir.

SCHNAPPY SHILLELAGH

2 parts Carolans Irish Cream

1 part DeKuyper Peppermint Schnapps

Stir well over ice.

SCORPION

½ part Vox Vodka

½ part DeKuyper Blackberry Brandy

1 part Rose's Grenadine

Combine in a shot glass.

SCOTCH 'N' SODA

2 oz. Dewar's White Label Scotch

3 oz. Club Soda

Stir with ice.

SCOTCH SMOOTHIE

1 oz. Coco Lopez Real Cream of Coconut

1¼ oz. Dewar's White Label Scotch

½ oz. Carolans Irish Cream

½ oz. DeKuyper Creme de Almond Liqueur

2 scoops Vanilla ice cream

Blend.

SCOTCH SOUR

1¼ oz. Dewar's White Label Scotch

1 oz. Lemon Juice

1 tsp. Sugar

Stir in a mixing glass and pour into a rocks glass with ice. Garnish with a Cherry and an Orange Slice.

SCOTTISH ICED TEA

One part Drambuie in a tall glass of freshly brewed unsweetened iced tea, garnished with lemon or a sprig of mint. Iced cold, a fantastic idea.

SCOTTY DOG

2 oz. Dewar's White Label

1½ oz. Rose's Lime Juice

Shake with ice and strain into a glass. Garnish with slice of lime.

SCREAMING SOUR APPLES

1¼ oz. Vox Vodka

¾ oz. DeKuyper Sour Apple Pucker

2½ oz. Sweet & sour mix

Shake and serve in a tall glass.

SCREWDRIVER

1¼ oz. Vox Vodka

4 oz. Orange Juice

Add Vox Vodka to a tall glass with ice and fill with Orange Juice.

SCREWY APPLE

1¼ oz. DeKuyper Sour Apple Pucker

3 oz. Orange juice

Serve in a tall glass.

SEA BREEZE

2 oz. Vox Vodka

2 oz. Cranberry juice

2 oz. Grapefruit juice

Shake ingredients with ice and strain into ice-filled glass.

SEA DIPPER

1½ oz. Bacardi Light Rum

1 oz. Pineapple Juice

¼ oz. Rose's Lime Juice

1 tsp. Powdered Sugar

Shake with ice and serve over ice.

SECRET PLACE

1½ oz. Bacardi Dark Rum

½ oz. DeKuyper Cherry Brandy

2 tsp. DeKuyper Dark Crème de Cacao

4 oz. Cold Coffee

Stir with crushed ice and serve in a tall glass.

SEE-THRU

2 oz. Bombay Sapphire Gin

Pour over lots of ice.

SEX ON THE BEACH

¾ oz. Chambord

¾ oz. DeKuyper Melon Liqueur

2 oz. Pineapple Juice

splash Cranberry Juice

Combine in a mixing glass. Shake or stir. Pour in a shot glass. You can also serve this one over ice in a rocks glass.

SEX ON THE BEACH
(SOUTHERN STYLE)

½ oz. DeKuyper Sour Apple Pucker

½ oz. DeKuyper Peachtree Schnapps

½ oz. Cranberry juice

½ oz. Pineapple juice

Shake or stir. Pour in a shot glass.

SHAMROCK COCKTAIL

1½ oz. Tullamore Dew Irish Whiskey

½ oz. Martini & Rossi Dry Vermouth

¼ oz. DeKuyper Green Crème de Menthe

Stir well with cracked ice and strain or serve over ice. Garnish with an olive.

SHAMROCK COCKTAIL II

1½ oz. Tullamore Dew Irish Whiskey

¾ oz. DeKuyper Green Crème de Menthe

4 oz. Vanilla Ice Cream

Blend. Pour into a chilled wine goblet.

SHETLAND PONY

1½ oz. Dewar's Scotch

¾ oz. Irish Mist

dash Orange Bitters

Mix all ingredients with cracked ice and strain into a chilled cocktail glass. You can also serve this drink over ice.

SHORE BREEZE

1½ oz. Bacardi Light Rum

3 oz. Pineapple Juice

2 oz. Cranberry Juice

2 dashes Angostura

Shake with ice and serve in a rocks glass.

SHOOTER, SLAMMER OR MUPPET

1 part Jose Cuervo Especial

1 part 7-Up

Pour Jose Cuervo Especial and 7-Up into a shot glass. Hold the filled glass with your palm firmly covering the top of the glass so the liquid does not spill out when you slam it onto the table, hard. After slamming, immediately shoot it all at once.

SIBERIAN SUNRISE

1½ oz. Vox Vodka

4 oz. Grapefruit Juice

½ oz. Cointreau

Mix all ingredients with cracked ice in a shaker or blend.

SICILIAN KISS

2 parts Southern Comfort

1 part Disaronno Amaretto

Pour over crushed ice in short glasses, stir.

SIDECAR

1½ oz. Hennessy VS

¾ oz. Cointreau

¾ tsp. Fresh Lemon Juice

Combine all ingredients in a shaker and shake vigorously. Strain into chilled cocktail glass, with sugar rim.

SIDECAR IN BOMBAY

1½ oz. Bombay Sapphire
        Gin

¼ oz. Cointreau

¼ oz. Lemon Juice

Shake with ice and serve on
the rocks or up in a sugar-
rimmed glass.

SIESTA

1½ oz. Jose Cuervo Tequila

¾ oz. Lime Juice

½ oz. Bombay Sapphire
       Gin

Shake with ice and strain into
a chilled cocktail glass.

SILK PANTIES

1 part Vox Vodka

1 part DeKuyper Peachtree
        Schnapps

Combine in a shot glass.

Sandra Gutierrez
Chicago, Illinois

SILVER BULLET MARTINI

1½ oz. Vox Vodka

dash Martini & Rossi
      Extra Dry Vermouth

splash Dewar's Scotch

Stir the first two ingredients
gently over ice and strain.
Float Dewar's on top.

SIMPLY BONKERS

1 oz. Chambord

1 oz. Bacardi Rum

1 oz. Cream

Combine in a shot glass.

SINGAPORE SLING

1 oz. Bombay Sapphire Gin

½ oz. DeKuyper Cherry Brandy

3 dashes Benedictine

dash Rose's Grenadine

½ oz. Sweetened Lemon Mix

Club soda

Shake first five ingredients and pour into a tall glass. Top with club soda.

SLIM JIM

1¼ oz. Vox Vodka

3 oz. Diet soda

In a highball glass with ice, fill with diet soda. Garnish with lemon or lime slice.

SLIM BOMBAY SAPPHIRE GIN

1½ oz. Bombay Sapphire Gin

2 oz. Diet Soda

In a tall glass filled with ice and your favorite diet soda.

SLOE BOMBAY SAPPHIRE GIN FIZZ

1 oz. DeKuyper Sloe Gin

1 oz. Bombay Sapphire Gin

1½ oz. Sweet & Sour mix

Club soda

Shake, pour with ice into 12 oz. fizz glass and fill with soda. Maraschino cherry garnish.

SLOE BOMBAY SAPPHIRE GIN FIZZ II

1½ oz.   Bombay Sapphire Gin

3 oz.   Sweetened Lemon Mix

Club Soda

Shake Bombay Sapphire Gin and Lemon Mix and pour into a glass. Top with Club Soda.

SMOOTH PINK LEMONADE

1½ oz.   Vox Vodka

2 oz.   Cranberry juice

2 oz.   Sour mix

½ oz.   7-Up

Shake and serve in a tall glass over ice.

SNOW DROP

¼ oz.   Cointreau

¼ oz.   Liquore Galliano

¼ oz.   Vox Vodka

¼ oz.   DeKuyper White Crème de Cacao

1 oz.   Cream

Shake with ice and strain.

SOGGY CHERRY

2 oz.   DeKuyper Cheri-Beri Pucker

3   Slightly crushed Maraschino cherries

Fill with soda.

SOL-A-RITA

1¼ oz. Jose Cuervo Gold
       Tequila

¾ oz. Cointreau

1½ oz. Orange Juice

2 dashes Rose's Grenadine

Shake or blend. Serve up or
on the rocks.

SOPHISTICATE

1 oz. Bacardi O™

½ oz. DeKuyper Melon
      Liqueur

½ oz. Lemon/Lime Soda

½ oz. Cranberry Juice

Serve over ice. Garnish with
melon, strawberry and sugar-
coated orange.

SOUR APPLE MARGARITA

2 oz. DeKuyper Sour
     Apple Pucker

1 oz. Jose Cuervo Tequila

½ oz. Lime juice

3 oz. Sweet & sour mix

Shake or blend. Serve in salted
rimmed glass.

SOUR APPLE PUCKER DRIVER

Fill tall glass with ice and
orange juice. Pour DeKuyper
Sour Apple Pucker on top. Let
filter down through the juice,
stir.

SOUR APPLE PUCKER POPSICLE

2 oz. DeKuyper Sour
     Apple Pucker

1 cup Vanilla ice cream

Blend.

SOUR APPLE SNOW CONES

2 oz. DeKuyper Sour
     Apple Pucker

Served over crushed ice.

SOUR APPLE SPORTIER

1½ oz. DeKuyper Sour
      Apple Pucker

½ oz. Vox Vodka

2 oz. 7-Up

Stir with ice in a tall glass.

SOUR APPLE SPRITZER

1½ oz. DeKuyper Sour
      Apple Pucker

½ oz. Vox Vodka

2 oz. Club Soda

Stir with ice in a tall glass.
Top with club soda.

SOUR APPLETINI

Equal parts DeKuyper Sour
Apple Pucker, Vox Vodka,
Splash of sweet & sour mix,
Chill, strain, serve in a Martini
glass. Garnish with apple slice.

SOUR KISSES MARTINI

1½ oz. Bombay Sapphire
      Gin

dash Martini & Rossi
      Extra Dry Vermouth

½ oz. DeKuyper Sour
      Apple Pucker

Stir. Strain into martini glass.

SOUTH FORK COFFEE

1½ oz. Knob Creek Bourbon

½ oz. DeKuyper Dark Creme de Cacao

3 oz. Coffee

Add Knob Creek Bourbon and DeKuyper Dark Creme de Cacao to coffee.

SOUTHERN ALEXANDER

1½ oz. Southern Comfort

1½ oz. DeKuyper Dark Creme de Cacao

½ oz. Cream

1 cup ice

Blend.

SOUTHERN FROST

1½ oz. Southern Comfort

2 oz. Cranberry juice

2 oz. Ginger Ale

Fill tall glass with ice. Add all ingredients and stir.

SOUTHERN LADY

2 oz. Knob Creek Bourbon

½ oz. Southern Comfort

½ oz. DeKuyper Creme de Almond

3 oz. Pineapple Juice

1 oz. Lime Juice

2 oz. Lemon-Lime Soda

Shake first four ingredients with ice and strain into hurricane glass half-filled with ice. Fill with soda. Top with lime juice. Garnish with pineapple wheel and Maraschino cherry.

SOUTHERN PEACH

1¾ oz. Knob Creek Bourbon

1 oz. DeKuyper Peachtree Schnapps

⅛ oz. Grenadine

2 oz. Orange Juice

2 oz. Sour Mix

Fill parfait or hurricane glass with ice. Pour grenadine over ice; add Bourbon. Pour orange juice, sour mix, and Schnapps and shake. Garnish with a peach slice.

SOUTHERN PINK FLAMINGO

2 oz. Southern Comfort

½ oz. Bacardi Rum

2 oz. Pineapple juice

splash Rose's Grenadine

1 oz. Lemon juice

Shake and serve over ice.

SOUTHERN SHAG

1½ oz. Southern Comfort

2 oz. Cranberry juice

½ oz. Orange juice

Stir and garnish with a lime wedge.

SOUTHERN TRADITIONAL MARGARITA

1½ oz. Jose Cuervo Gold Tequila

⅝ oz. Southern Comfort

5 oz. Sweet & Sour Mix

½ oz. Fresh Lime Juice

Combine in a tall glass over ice. Garnish with a Lime Wedge.

SPANISH MARTINI

1½ oz. Bombay Sapphire
Gin

½ oz. Spanish Sherry

Shake with ice and strain into
a chilled martini glass.
Garnish with a lemon twist.

SPEARAMISTY

1 oz. Irish Mist

¼ oz. DeKuyper
Spearmint Schnapps

Stir ingredients and serve
straight up or over ice.

SPIKE

1½ oz. Jose Cuervo Gold
Tequila

4 oz. Grapefruit Juice

Combine in a highball glass.

SPIRITED
COFFEE LOPEZ

½ oz. Coco Lopez Real
Cream of Coconut

8 oz. Hot coffee

½ oz. Tullamore Dew
Irish Whiskey

Whipped cream as desired.
Serve in coffee mug.

SPRING FLING

Equal parts DeKuyper Cheri-
Beri Pucker, Grape Pucker,
Mad Melon, San Tropique
over ice with orange juice,
pineapple juice and top with
cranberry juice, shake and
serve.

SPRITZER

3 oz. Dry White Wine

Club Soda

Pour Wine in a glass and fill
with Soda. Garnish with a
Lemon Twist.

ST. PATRICK'S DAY COCKTAIL

¾ oz. Tullamore Dew Irish Whiskey

¾ oz. DeKuyper Green Creme de Menthe

¾ oz. Green Chartreuse

1 dash Angostura bitters

Stir. Serve over ice.

STAIRCASE

¼ oz. Drambuie

1 oz. Dewar's Scotch

¼ oz. Martini & Rossi Dry Vermouth

¼ oz. Martini & Rossi Rosso Vermouth

Serve in rocks glass with ice.

STEAMBOAT SPECIAL

¼ oz. Cointreau

1 oz. Dewar's Scotch

Float Cointreau over Dewar's Scotch in a shot glass.

STEEPLE JACK

1 oz. Laird's Applejack

2 oz. Rose's Lime Juice

Mix over ice in a short glass. Garnish with lime wedge.

STILETTO

1½ oz. Knob Creek Bourbon

1 oz. Disaronno Amaretto

Juice of ½ Lemon

Shake with ice. Pour into glass over ice cubes.

STINGER

2 oz. Hennessy Cognac

¾ oz. DeKuyper White
　　　Creme de Menthe

Shake with ice and strain into
chilled cocktail glass or
brandy snifter.

STOPLIGHT

2 oz. DeKuyper Sloe Gin

2 oz. Bombay Sapphire
　　　Gin

1 oz. Lemon juice

1 scoop Crushed ice

1 Maraschino cherry

Shake with ice. Strain the mixture into a chilled cocktail
glass. Garnish with
Maraschino cherry.

SUBMARINE

Jose Cuervo Especial

Beer

All the time in the
world

Fill a shot glass with Jose
Cuervo Especial. Very slowly
put the shot upside down
inside a beer mug, making
sure the Cuervo stays inside
the shot glass. Slowly fill the
mug with beer. Try not to mix
the Cuervo with the beer.
Drink it all in one shot.

SUNBURST

1¼ oz. Vox Vodka

dash Cointreau

2 oz. Grapefruit Juice

Serve in rocks glass over ice.
Add dash of Cointreau.

SUNSET MARTINI COCKTAIL

1½ oz. Bacardi O™

½ oz. Tropico Liqueur

3 oz. Lemonade

Shake with ice and strain into sugar-rimmed martini glass. Float Tropico Liqueur on top.

SUNSET PUNCH

1½ oz. Bacardi Light Rum

4 oz. Orange juice

½ oz. Rose's Lime Juice

½ oz. Rose's Grenadine

Shake Bacardi Light Rum, orange juice and Rose's Lime Juice. Pour into a tall glass filled with ice. Spoon in Rose's Grenadine.

SUPER O MARTINI COCKTAIL

2 oz. Bacardi O™

1 oz. Tropico Liqueur

¼ oz. Bombay Sapphire Gin

¼ oz. Cointreau

Shake; serve in chilled glass with orange garnish.

SUPER MARTINI COCKTAIL

1 oz. Bacardi O™

¼ oz. Rose's Grenadine

¼ oz. Orange Juice

Shake with ice; strain into a chilled martini glass.

SURE BOMBAY SAPPHIRE GIN FIZZ

2 oz. Bombay Sapphire Gin

2 oz. Sweetened Lemon Mix

      Club Soda

Shake with ice. Serve in a tall glass filled with ice. Top with club soda.

SWAMP WATER

¾ oz. Cointreau

¾ oz. Green Chartreuse

½ oz. Pineapple Juice

Shake with ice and strain.

SWEET & SOUR APPLETINI

1 oz. DeKuyper Sour Apple Pucker

1 oz. Vox Vodka

splash Sweet & sour mix

Shake with ice, strain and serve in a chilled martini glass.

SWEET TART

1 oz. Vox Vodka

¼ oz. Chambord

¼ oz. Rose's Lime Juice

¼ oz. Pineapple Juice

Shake with ice and strain into a shot glass.

SWEET MARTINI

2 oz. Bombay Sapphire Gin

¾ oz. Martini & Rossi Rosso Vermouth

Stir with ice and serve over rocks or strain into a chilled martini glass. Garnish with an orange twist.

SWEETEST TABOO

1 oz. Campari

1 oz. Cointreau

1½ oz. Bombay Sapphire
Gin

Orange juice

Pour Campari, Cointreau and
Bombay Sapphire Gin into a
glass with ice. Fill with orange
juice. Stir.

TANGO MARTINI
COCKTAIL

2 oz. Bacardi O™

½ oz. Chambord

½ oz. Cointreau

1 oz. Pineapple Juice

splash Cranberry Juice

Shake with ice; strain into
chilled martini glass. Squeeze
orange in bottom of glass;
garnish with an orange twist.

TARZAN O'REILLY

1 oz. Carolans Irish Cream

1 oz. Vox Vodka

1 oz. DeKuyper Creme
de Banana

Stir. Serve on the rocks.

TEA WITH LOVE

2 oz. Disaronno
Amaretto

6 oz. Hot tea

Top with chilled whipped
cream. Serve in a mug.

TEQUADOR

1½ oz. Jose Cuervo Tequila

2 oz. Pineapple Juice

1 dash Rose's Lime Juice

Rose's Grenadine

Shake the first three ingredi-
ents with crushed ice. Strain.
Add a few drops of Rose's
Grenadine.

TEQUILA GIMLET

1½ oz. Jose Cuervo Tequila

1½ oz. Rose's Lime Juice

Blend Cuervo and Lime Juice with crushed ice and pour into a glass. Garnish with a Lime Wheel or Green Cherry.

TEQUILA JULEP

1¼ oz. Jose Cuervo Tequila

1 tsp. Superfine Sugar

2 sprigs Fresh Mint

Club Soda

Crush three Mint Leaves with sugar in a chilled highball glass and fill with ice. Add Cuervo and top with Club Soda. Garnish with a Sprig of Mint.

TEQUILA SUNRISE

1½ oz. Jose Cuervo Tequila

½ oz. Rose's Grenadine

Orange Juice

Pour Rose's Grenadine into a tall glass first. Then add Cuervo and fill with ice and Orange Juice. Garnish with an Orange Slice.

TEQUILA TEASER

1½ oz. Jose Cuervo Tequila

½ oz. Cointreau

1½ oz. Orange Juice

½ oz. Grapefruit Juice

Pour ingredients into a tall glass filled with ice.

TEQUINA

2 oz. Jose Cuervo Tequila

½ oz. Martini & Rossi Dry Vermouth

Stir Cuervo and Vermouth with ice in a mixing glass until chilled. Strain into a chilled cocktail glass and garnish with a Lemon Twist.

THE BACARDI FIZZLE

1 oz. Bacardi Razz

splash Cointreau

1½ oz. Cranberry juice

Shake ingredients with ice. Pour into tall glass. Top with Sprite.

THE BIG APPLE

1½ oz. DeKuyper Sour Apple Pucker

½ oz. Rose's Grenadine

½ oz. Lemon juice

Serve over ice.

THE BOMB

Equal parts:

DeKuyper Grape Pucker

DeKuyper Cheri-Beri Pucker

DeKuyper Sour Apple Pucker

DeKuyper BluesBerry

DeKuyper Mad Melon

Vox Vodka

Cranberry Juice

Shake and serve in a tall glass or strain into a shot glass.

THE CUERVO SHOT

1 oz. Jose Cuervo Especial

pinch Salt

Lime Wedge

Pour Jose Cuervo Especial into a shot glass. Lick the skin between your thumb and forefinger and sprinkle salt on the moist skin. Drink the tequila (all at once, quickly), lick the salt and suck on the lime.

THE LONDON MARTINI

2 oz. Bombay Sapphire Gin

½ oz. Martini & Rossi Rosso Vermouth

½ oz. DeKuyper Blue Curacao

splash Pineapple Juice

Mix all ingredients with cracked ice in shaker; strain into martini glass.

THE S.O.S.

3 parts Bacardi O™

1 part Chambord

2 parts Sweet and sour mix

1 part Cranberry juice

Shake all ingredients with ice and strain into shot glass.

THOROUGHBRED COOLER

1 oz. Knob Creek Bourbon

1 oz. Orange Juice

dash Rose's Grenadine

Lemon-Lime Soda

Pour all ingredients over ice in highball glass. Fill with lemon-lime soda and stir. Add dash of grenadine; garnish with an orange wedge.

TIDAL WAVE

1½ oz.   Laird's Applejack

4 oz.   Orange Juice

splash   Cranberry Juice

Pour Laird's AppleJack over ice in a tall glass. Add orange juice and splash of cranberry juice. Garnish with slice of orange.

TIPPERARY COCKTAIL

¾ oz.   Tullamore Dew Irish Whiskey

¾ oz.   Green Chartreuse

¾ oz.   Martini & Rossi Dry Vermouth

Stir well with cracked ice and strain into cocktail glass.

TO THE MOON

1 oz.   Carolans Irish Cream

1 oz.   Disaronno Amaretto

½ oz.   DeKuyper Coffee Liqueur

¼ oz.   Bacardi Rum (151-proof)

Serve in a shot glass.

TOASTED ALMOND

1 oz.   DeKuyper Coffee Liqueur

½ oz.   Disaronno Amaretto

1 oz.   Cream or Milk

Pour over ice and stir.

TOASTED IRISHMAN

1 part   Irish Mist

1 part   DeKuyper Coffee Liqueur

1 part   Disaronno Amaretto

Shake with ice and serve on the rocks.

TOM & JERRY

1 oz. Bacardi Light Rum

¼ oz. Bacardi Select Rum

1 Egg

1 tsp. Sugar

Separate yolk from white of egg and beat each separately. When white is fairly stiff, add sugar and beat to a stiff froth, combine white and yolk. Put rums in mug, add boiling water, 1 Tbsp. of egg mixture and sprinkle with nutmeg.

TOM COLLINS

2 oz. Bombay Sapphire Gin

2 oz. Sweetened Lemon Mix

Club Soda

Shake Bombay and lemon mix with ice, fill tall glass. Add club soda. Garnish with Maraschino cherry and orange slice.

TOPAZ MARTINI

1¾ oz. Bacardi Limón

¼ oz. Martini & Rossi Extra Dry Vermouth

splash DeKuyper Blue Curacao

Combine in a cocktail glass.

Heart and Soul
San Francisco, CA

TRAIL BLAZE

1 oz. Drambuie

1 oz. Chambord

1 oz. Sweet & Sour Mix

Shake with ice. Serve over ice.

TRANSFUSION

1¼ oz. Vox Vodka

3 oz. Grape juice

In a tall glass with ice, fill with grape juice. Top with club soda (optional).

TROPICAL APPLE PIE

1¼ oz. DeKuyper Sour
          Apple Pucker

2 scoops Vanilla ice cream

¼ oz. Scoop ice

2 wedge Cored apple

2 oz. Coco Lopez Cream
      of Coconut

Blend. Serve in a tall glass.

TROPICAL APPLE PUNCH

1½ oz. DeKuyper Sour
          Apple Pucker

½ oz. DeKuyper San
        Tropique

3 oz. Cranberry juice

3 oz. Orange juice

Serve in a tall glass.

TROPICAL APPLE PUNCH II

1½ oz. DeKuyper Sour
          Apple Pucker

½ oz. Bacardi Còco

3 oz. Cranberry juice

3 oz. Orange juice

Serve in a tall glass.

TROPICAL BREEZE

1 oz. Coco Lopez Cream
      of Coconut

2 oz. Orange Juice

1 oz. Bacardi Rum

½ oz. DeKuyper Crème de
        Banana

Blend. Garnish with a
Pineapple Slice.

TROPICAL RENDEZVOUS

2 parts DeKuyper Tropical
Pineapple Schnapps

1 part DeKuyper Peachtree
Schnapps

Fill with lemon-lime soda
over ice in tall glass.

TROPICAL STORM

1½ oz. Cointreau

1½ oz. DeKuyper Creme de
Banana Liqueur

1 oz. Lime or lemon juice

Mint leaves

Cherry

Shake lime (or lemon juice),
DeKuyper Banana Liqueur
and Cointreau with ice. Strain
into a tumbler glass full of ice.
Stir. Garnish with mint leaves,
Maraschino cherry and lime
slice.

TRUE BLUE

½ part Jose Cuervo Especial

½ part Vox Vodka

½ part DeKuyper Blue
Curacao

Pour all ingredients into a
cocktail shaker with crushed
ice and shake well. Strain into
a chilled shot glass.

TULLAMORE DEW HOT IRISH TEA

1½ oz. Tullamore Dew Irish
Whiskey

4 oz. Hot Tea

In a mug stir the ingredients
well. Add a Cinnamon Stick.

TULLAMORE DEW IRISH COOLER

1 jigger Tullamore Dew Irish
Whiskey

1 pint Club soda

1 dash Angostura bitters

1 Lemon rind

Serve in a tall glass.

TUSCAN RED SANGRIA

1 750ml bottle Martini & Rossi Extra Dry Vermouth

2 cups Cranberry juice cocktail

½ cup Hennessy Cognac

½ cup Sugar

2 Oranges, halved and thinly sliced

1 Lemon, halved and thinly sliced

2 cups Chilled sparkling water

Combine Martini & Rossi Extra Dry Vermouth, cranberry juice, cognac and sugar in a large pitcher; stir until sugar is dissolved. Chill until ready to serve. Stir in sliced fruit and sparkling water. Serve over ice. Makes 8⅓ cups.

ULTIMATE IRISH COFFEE

1½ oz. Irish Mist

Hot coffee

Topped with whipped cream. No sugar needed.

ULTIMATE MARTINI

3 oz. Bombay Sapphire Gin

1 oz. Martini & Rossi Extra Dry Vermouth

1-2 dashes Orange Bitters (or orange peel)

Garnish with 1 cocktail olive and twist of lemon. Shake or stir. Serve in classic martini glass.

ULTIMATE PUCKER

1 part DeKuyper
        Watermelon Pucker

1 part DeKuyper Sour
        Apple Pucker

Chill, serve as a shot.

ULTIMATE TEA

1½ oz. Irish Mist

3 oz. Hot tea

       Bit of lemon

Serve in a mug.

ULTIMATE
VOX VODKA
MARTINI

1 oz. Vox Vodka

½ oz. Campari

¼ oz. Martini & Rossi
       Rosso Vermouth

Shake with ice, strain into a
chilled martini glass.

URBAN COCKTAIL

1 oz. Vox Vodka

¾ oz. Hpnotiq

¼ oz. Bacardi Light Rum

splash Cointreau

splash Citris

*Metrodome
NY, NY*

UTOPIA: IN THE
GRANITA STYLE

½ glass Blueberries
         raspberries &
         strawberries

2 tsps. Fine sugar

¾ oz. Chambord

       Champagne

Shake. Champagne to top.

VANILLA APPLES

1¼ oz. DeKuyper Sour
        Apple Pucker

¾ oz. DeKuyper Thrilla
        Vanilla

½ oz. Rose's Grenadine

2 oz. Sweet & sour mix

Top with orange juice. Serve
in a tall glass with ice.

VANILLA RILLA

¾ oz. Bacardi Vaníl

¾ oz. Bacardi Razz

5 oz. Cranberry Juice

Pour ingredients over ice. Stir.
Serve in a tall glass.

VANILA ROSE

1 oz. Bacardi Vaníl

½ oz. DeKuyper Wild
        Strawberry Liqueur

splash Rose's Grenadine

1½ oz. Cream

Serve in a rocks glass on ice.
Garnish with a Maraschino
cherry.

Luzi Galvan
Lalo's
Chicago, IL

VICIOUS SID

1½ oz. Bacardi Light Rum

½ oz. Southern Comfort

½ oz. Cointreau

1 oz. Lemon Juice

1 dash Bitters

Shake ingredients with ice and
serve over ice.

VOO-DOO DOLL MARTINI

1½ oz. Bacardi Razz

½ oz. Chambord

1 oz. Cranberry juice

splash Sour mix

Garnish with fresh strawberries.

Belin Jackson
Blue Bayou
Chicago, IL

VOX AND TONIC

2 oz. Vox Vodka

3 oz. Tonic

Pour Vox Vodka over ice in tall glass. Fill with tonic. Add squeeze of lime.

VOX BRAVO

½ oz. Vox Vodka

½ oz. Campari

Pour Vox Vodka and Campari over ice in a tall glass. Top with tonic. Garnish with a slice of lemon and a slice of lime.

VOX COLLINS

2 oz. Vox Vodka

¾ oz. Sweetened Lemon Mix

Club Soda

Shake with ice and pour in tall glass with ice. Fill with club soda.

VOX GIMLET

2 oz. Vox Vodka

½ oz. Fresh Lime Juice

Mix Vox Vodka and lime juice in a glass with ice. Strain and serve in cocktail glass. Garnish with a twist of lime.

VOX
ISLAND ROCKER

3 oz. Vox Vodka

1 oz. DeKuyper Melon Liqueur

3 oz. Orange Juice

Shake with ice strain into a martini glass. Garnish with orange slice.

VOX MADRAS

2 oz. Vox Vodka

2 oz. Orange Juice

2 oz. Cranberry Juice

In a tall glass with ice, fill with half orange juice, half cranberry juice.

VOX
BULL SHOT

1¼ oz. Vox Vodka

5 oz. Beef Consomme

5 dashes Worcestershire Sauce

1 tps. Lemon Juice

Pinch Celery Salt or Seed

Mix ingredients with ice in a tall glass. Pepper to taste.

VOX SALT
AND PEPPER

1¼ oz. Vox Vodka

Pour chilled Vox Vodka into a salt-rimmed cocktail glass. Garnish with a cucumber spear. Pepper to taste.

VOX
SALTY DOG

$1\frac{1}{2}$ oz. Vox Vodka

$\frac{3}{4}$ oz. Grapefruit Juice

$\frac{1}{4}$ tsp. Salt

Coat rim of glass with salt.
Mix and pour on the rocks.

VOX
SCREWDRIVER

Vox Vodka and freshly-
squeezed orange juice mixed
over ice. In a tall glass.

VOX
SEABREEZE

$1\frac{1}{4}$ oz. Vox Vodka

2 oz. Cranberry Juice

2 oz. Grapefruit Juice

Pour Vox Vodka over ice in a
tall glass. Fill half way with
grapefruit juice and top it off
with cranberry juice.

VOX VODKA
MARTINI

$1\frac{1}{2}$ oz. Vox Vodka

dash Martini & Rossi
Extra Dry Vermouth

Stir. Strain and serve straight
up or on the rocks with some
ice in cocktail glass. Add
lemon twist or olive.

VOX WHITE BERRY

3 oz. Vox Vodka

1 oz. Cointreau

splash Fresh Lime Juice

Shake with ice, strain into martini glass. Garnish with a Raspberry.

VOX WHITE RUSSIAN

1 oz. Vox Vodka

$\frac{1}{2}$ oz. Chocolate Liqueur

Heavy Cream

Pour Vox Vodka, Chocolate Liqueur and cream over ice in a rocks glass. Shake and serve.

WARD EIGHT

$1\frac{1}{4}$ oz. Knob Creek Bourbon

4 dashes Rose's Grenadine

Juice of $\frac{1}{2}$ Lemon

Shake ingredients with cracked ice and strain into a glass with finely cracked ice.

WARDEN MARTINI

$1\frac{1}{2}$ oz. Bombay Sapphire Gin

dash Martini & Rossi Extra Dry Vermouth

dash Pernod

Stir in cocktail glass. Strain & serve straight up or on the rocks. Add lemon twist or olives.

WASHINGTON APPLE

2 parts Knob Creek Bourbon

1 part DeKuyper Sour Apple Pucker

2 parts Cranberry juice

Served in a martini glass with a Maraschino cherry.

WATERBABY

1 part DeKuyper Watermelon Pucker

2 parts Pineapple juice

Serve in tall glass with crushed ice.

WATERMELON AND STRAWBERRY MARGARITA

1½ parts Jose Cuervo Especial

3 parts Jose Cuervo Margarita Mix

1½ cups (packed) frozen Chopped Seeded Watermelon

½ cup (packed) frozen quartered Unsweetened Strawberries

½ Tbs. Sugar

Pinch Salt

Watermelon Wedge

Puree all ingredients (except watermelon wedge) in blender until smooth. Pour into chilled margarita glass. Garnish with watermelon wedge.

WATERMELON FIZZ

2 parts DeKuyper Watermelon Pucker

Fill glass with 7-up. Serve over ice in a tall glass.

WATERMELON MARTINI

2 cups Cubed watermelon flesh

2 parts Vox Vodka

¼ part sugar syrup

½ part DeKuyper

Muddle watermelon in base of shaker, add other ingredients; shake with ice and strain into glass.

WATER MELONTINI

1 part DeKuyper
     Watermelon Pucker

1 part Vox Vodka

Garnish with watermelon slice.

WAVE BREAKER

³⁄₄ oz. Vox Vodka

¹⁄₂ oz. Cointreau

¹⁄₈ oz. Lime Juice

³⁄₄ oz. Coco Lopez Real
     Cream of Coconut

Blend with ice and strain.

WEEKEND AT THE BEACH

1 oz. DeKuyper Sour
     Apple Pucker

1 oz. DeKuyper Peachtree
     Schnapps

2 oz. Pineapple juice

2 oz. Cranberry juice

Shake with ice. Serve up or
over ice.

WET KISS

1 part DeKuyper
     Watermelon Pucker

¹⁄₂ part Disaronno Amaretto

splash Lemon

Chill, and serve as a shot.

WHISKEY SOUR

1¹⁄₂ oz. Knob Creek
     Bourbon

³⁄₄ oz. Sweetened Lemon
     Juice

1 tsp. Superfine Sugar

Shake with ice. Serve straight
up or over ice.

WHISPER

½ oz. Martini & Rossi Dry
Vermouth

Grated lime or
lemon peel

1 oz. Vox Vodka

1 oz. Cointreau

Pour dry vermouth, Vox Vodka
and Cointreau into a mixing
glass with ice. Stir. Strain into
a cocktail glass.

WHISPER MARTINI

1½ oz. Vox Vodka

1 or 2 drops Martini & Rossi
Dry Vermouth

Garnish to taste.

WHITE LADY

2 parts Bombay Sapphire
Gin

1 part Cointreau

1 part Sweetened Lemon
Mix

Shake well with ice and serve
on the rocks.

WHITE RUSSIAN

Pour 1½ parts DeKuyper
Coffee Liqueur, 1 part Vox
Vodka over ice. Top with 1½
parts cream. Shake with ice.
Serve up or on ice.

WIDOW MAKER

½ oz. Drambuie

1 oz. Knob Creek Bourbon

½ oz. Dewar's Scotch

1 oz. Lemon Juice

1 oz. Orange Juice

In an old-fashioned glass, shake with ice, strain over ice.

WILD IRISH ROSE

1½ oz. Tullamore Dew Irish Whiskey

1½ tsp. Rose's Grenadine

½ oz. Rose's Lime Juice

Club soda

Fill a highball glass with ice. Add Tullamore Dew Irish Whiskey, grenadine and lime juice. Stir well. Fill with club soda.

WILD ROVER

1 part Carolans Irish Cream Liqueur

1 part Irish Mist

Serve on the rocks.

WINTER WARM-UP

2 oz. Chambord

½ oz. DeKuyper Coffee Liqueur

3 oz. Hot coffee

Whipped cream

Serve in a coffee cup or mug.

WOLF HOUND

1 oz. Tullamore Dew Irish Whiskey

¾ oz. DeKuyper Dark Crème de Cacao

½ oz. Half & Half

splash Club Soda

Stir ingredients with ice and serve over ice.

WOO
WOO

¾ oz. Vox Vodka

¾ oz. DeKuyper
Peppermint
Schnapps

Shake with ice. Serve in a shot
glass or over ice.

WOODY
MELON

2 shots DeKuyper
Watermelon Pucker

½ shot Knob Creek
Bourbon

Squeeze of lemon

Shake and serve over ice.

YELLOW
BIRD

¾ oz. Bacardi Rum

¼ oz. Liquore Galliano

¼ oz. DeKuyper Crème de
Banana

2 oz. Pineapple Juice

2 oz. Orange juice

Shake. Serve in a tall glass.

YELLOW
FELLOW

1 oz. Bombay Sapphire
Gin

¼ oz. Yellow Chartreuse

Shake. Strain into cocktail
glass.

YUCATAN MARGARITA WITH TROPICAL FRUIT

1½ parts Jose Cuervo Especial

3 parts Jose Cuervo Margarita Mix

1 Tbs. Papaya Nectar

1 Tbs. Guava Nectar

1 Tbs. Cream of Coconut

Lime Slice

Lime Wedge

Sugar

Rub rim of margarita glass with lime wedge. Dip rim into sugar. Combine Jose Cuervo Especial, Jose Cuervo Margarita Mix, papaya nectar, guava nectar, cream of coconut and ice in mixing glass. Shake well. Pour into margarita glass. Garnish with lime slice.

ZOMBIE

¾ oz. Bacardi Light Rum

¼ oz. Bacardi Dark Rum

¼ tsp. Bacardi 151 Rum

1 oz. Pineapple Juice

1 oz. Orange Juice

1 oz. Lemon or Rose's Lime Juice

Mix the first two Rums and all Juices with ice in a shaker or blender and pour into a tall glass. Float ¼ tsp. Bacardi 151, garnish with a Pineapple Spear and a Maraschino Cherry.

Non-Alcoholic Cocktails

BANANA LOPEZ

2 oz. Coco Lopez Real
Cream of Coconut

1 Med. Banana

1 tsp. Lemon Juice

1 cup Ice

Mix in blender until smooth.

COCO LOPEZ SHAKE

2½ oz. Coco Lopez Real
Cream of Coconut

1 scoop Vanilla Ice Cream

1 cup Ice

Mix in a blender until
smooth.

DUST CUTTER

¾ oz. Rose's Lime Juice

6 oz. Schweppes Tonic
Water

Combine over ice in a tall
glass.

FLORIDA BANANA LOPEZ

2 oz. Coco Lopez Real
Cream of Coconut

4 oz. Orange Juice

1 Med. Banana

1 cup Ice

Mix in blender until smooth.

GRAPE LOPEZ

3 oz. Coco Lopez Real
Cream of Coconut

4 oz. Grape Juice

1½ cups Ice

Mix in blender until smooth.

NADA COLADA

1 oz. Coco Lopez Real
Cream of Coconut

2 oz. Pineapple Juice

1 cup Ice

Mix in blender until smooth.

ORANGE SMOOTHIE

2½ oz. Coco Lopez Real
Cream of Coconut

3 oz. Orange Juice

1 scoop Vanilla Ice Cream

1 cup Ice

Nutmeg

Mix in blender until smooth.
Sprinkle with nutmeg.

ORANGE SORBET LOPEZ

2 oz. Coco Lopez Real
Cream of Coconut

1 oz. Orange Juice

1 scoop Orange Sherbet

½ cup Ice

Mix in blender until smooth.

RUBY COOLER

1 cup Ocean Spray
Cranapple Juice
Drink

1 tsp. Instant Tea

Lemon Wedges

Mix together Cranapple Juice
and Tea. Pour over ice into
two tall glasses with lemon
wedge garnishes.

SHIRLEY TEMPLE

1 oz. Rose's Grenadine

5 oz. Schweppes Ginger Ale

Pour ingredients over ice in a tall glass. Garnish with Maraschino Cherry.

STRAWBERRY BANANA LOPEZ

2 oz. Coco Lopez Real Cream of Coconut

2 oz. Strawberries

½ Med. Banana

1 cup Ice

Mix in blender until smooth.

VIRGIN MARY

4 oz. Tomato Juice

dash Worcestershire Sauce

dash Tabasco Sauce

dash Salt and Pepper

dash Celery Salt

dash Soy Sauce

In a glass filled with ice, add Tomato Juice. Add a dash or two of Worcestershire Sauce, Tabasco, Salt and Pepper. Garnish with a celery stalk.

Resources

Not everyone is an expert and not all the information necessary can be found in just one book, so below I have included some resources that can answer any questions that you may have. First are the companies that make the fine liquors included in the recipes. Following that are other sources and a list of organizations that can help you as well:

Our Sponsors Websites

Bartender Magazine - www.Bartender.com

Bacardi - www.Bacardi.com

Bacardi O - www.BacardiO.com

Bombay Sapphire Gin - www.BombaySapphire.com

Carolans Irish Cream - www.Carolans.ie

Chambord - www.ChambordOnline.com

Cointreau - www.Cointreau.com

DeKuyper Cordials - www.DeKuyper.com

Dewars Scotch - www.Dewars.com

Disaronno Amaretto - www.Disaronno.com

Drambuie - www.Drambuie.com

Hennessy Cognac - www.Hennessy-Cognac.com

Irish Mist - www.IrishMist.com

Jim Beam Brands Worldwide - www.JimBeam.com

Jose Cuervo Tequila - www.Cuervo.com

Knob Creek Bourbon- www.KnobCreek.com

Martini & Rossi Vermouth - www.Martini.com

The Cherry Marketing Institute - www.CherryMKT.com

Tullamore Dew Irish Whiskey - www.Tullamore-Dew.com

Vox Vodka - www.VoxVodka.com

Other Sources

T-shirt and bar shirts - www.BarRags.com

Anheuser-Busch Beer Profits - www.BeerProfitGuide.com

Applejack - www.LairdAndCompany.com

Coco Lopez - www.CocoLopez.com

Precision Pour (Liquor Pourers) - www.PrecisionPour.com

Plastic and Fun Glasses - www.Top-ShelfMarketing.com

Automatic Frying Machines - www.AutoFry.com

Wine Racks - www.WineRacks.com

Pool Tables - www.BumperTube.com

Shelf Liners - www.Dri-Dek.com

Organizations

American Beverage Institute
1775 Pennsylvania Avenue NW, Suite 1200
Washington, DC 20006
(800) 843-8877; (202) 463-7110; FAX: (202) 463-7107
website: www.abionline.org
e-mail: abi@abionline.org

American Beverage Licensees
5101 River Road, Suite #108
Bethesda, MD 20816
(301) 656-1494; FAX: (301) 656-7539
website: www.ablusa.org
e-mail: info@ablusa.org

American Hotel And Lodging Association (AH&LA)
1201 New York Avenue NW, Suite 600
Washington, DC 20005-3931
(202) 289-3100; FAX: (202) 289-3199
website: www.ahla.com

Bartender Foundation
P.O. Box 158
Liberty Corner, NJ 07938
(908) 766-6006; FAX: (908) 766-6607
website: www.BartenderFoundation.com
e-mail: BarFound1@aol.com

Bartender Magazine
Foley Publishing Corp.
P.O. Box 158
Liberty Corner, NJ 07938
(908) 766-6006; FAX: (908) 766-6607
Jaclyn Wilson Foley, Editor
website: www.bartender.com
e-mail: barmag@aol.com

Beer Institute
122 C Street NW, Suite 750
Washington, DC 20001
1-800-379-BREW: FAX: (202) 737-7004
website: www.beerinstitute.org
e-mail: info@beerinstitute.org

Bureau Of Alcohol, Tobacco And Firearms (ATF)
Department of Treasury
650 Massachusetts Avenue
Washington, DC 20226
(202) 927-8100; FAX: (202) 927-8605
website: www.atf.treas.gov

California Association Of Winegrape Growers, (CAWG)
601 University Avenue, Suite 135
Sacramento, CA 95825
(916) 924-5370; FAX: (916) 924-5374
website: www.cawg.org
e-mail: info@cawg.org

Club Managers Association Of America (CMMA)
1733 King Street
Alexandria, VA 22314
(703) 739-9500; FAX: (703) 739-0124
website: www.cmaa.org
e-mail: cmaa@cmaa.org

Distilled Spirits Council of the United States
1250 Eye Street, NW, Suite 400
Washington, D.C. 20005
(202) 628-3544
website: www.discus.org

National Alcohol Beverage Control Association (NABCA)
4216 King Street West
Alexandria, VA 22302
(703) 578-4200; FAX: (703) 820-3551
website: www.nabca.org

National Association Of Beverage Importers, Inc. (NABI)
30 Courthouse Square, Suite 300
Rockville, MD 20850
(240) 453-9998; FAX: (240) 453-9358
website: www.nabi-inc.org
e-mail: beverageimporters@nabi-inc.org

National Association Of Wholesale-Distributors (NAW)
1725 K Street NW, Suite 300
Washington, DC 20006
(202) 872-0885; FAX: (202) 785-0586
website: www.naw.org
e-mail: naw@nawd.org

National Beer Wholesalers Association (NBWA)
1101 Kine Street
Alexandria, VA 22314-4494
(703) 683-4300; FAX: (703) 683-8965
website: www.nbwa.org
e-mail: info@nbwa.org

National Restaurant Association (NRA)
1200 17TH Street NW
Washington, DC 20036
(800) 424-5156; FAX: (202) 331-2429
website: www.restaurant.org

Society Of Wine Educators
1200 G Street NW, Suite 360
Washington, DC 20005
(202) 347-5677; FAX: (202) 347-5667
website: www.wine.gurus.com
e-mail: director@societyofwineeducators.org

Sopexa Food & Wine Marketing
80 Maiden Lane, Suite 310
New York, NY 10038
(212) 477-9800; FAX: (212) 473-4315
website: www.sopexa.com

The Food And Beverage Association Of America
666 Fifth Avenue
New York, NY 101803
(212) 344-8252; FAX: (973) 379-3117
website: www.fbassoc.com
e-mail: fbassociation@aol.com

The National Restaurant Association Educational Foundation
175 W. Jackson Boulevard, Suite 1500
Chicago, IL 60604
(800) 765-2122; FAX: (312) 258-1747
website: www.edfound.org

Wine Institute
425 Market Street, Suite 1000
San Francisco, CA 94105
(415) 512-0151; FAX: (415)442-0742
website: www.wineinstitute.org

Wines And Spirits Wholesalers Of America, Inc. (WSWA)
805 Fifteenth St. NW, Suite 430
Washington, DC 20005
(202) 371-9792; FAX: (202) 789-2405
website: www.wswa.org
e-mail: Karen.Grabois@wswa.org

Women Chefs & Restaurateurs (WCR)
304 W. Liberty Street, Suite 201
Louisville, KY 40202
(877) 927-7787; (502) 581-0300; FAX: (502) 589-3602
website: www.chefnet.com/WCR
e-mail: wcr@hqtrs.com

Women For Winesense
Sebastiani Vineyards
389 Fourth Street East
Sonoma, CA 95476
(707) 933-3205; FAX: (707) 933-3369
website: www.womenforwinesense.org
e-mail: info@womenforwinesense.org

World Association Of Alcohol Beverage Industries (WAABI)
P.O. Box 451057
Garland, TX 75045
(972) 675-3246; FAX: (972) 675-3673
website: www.waabi.org
e-mail: woodgateh@aol.com

Zinfandel Advocates & Producers (ZAP)
P.O. Box 1487
Rough & Ready, CA 95975
(530) 274-4900; FAX: (530) 274-4904
website: www.zinfandel.org
e-mail: zaprr@oro.net

Wine, Women and Cigar
20" x 26"

California Cuisine
18³/₄" x 26"

BARTENDER MAGAZINE

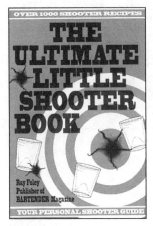

Contains just about
every shooter imaginable.
$10.95 (includes shipping)

Over 150 X-Rated
drink recipes.
$10.95 (includes shipping)

Over 300 quotes and advice
from one of the greatest
sources: Anonymous!
$10.95 (includes shipping)

Travel to Ireland via your tastebuds
and experience the many Spirits of Irish
Whisky, Malts, Stouts, and Cream
Liqueurs. $12.95 (includes shipping)

S PECIALTY I TEMS

Bar Signals Poster
23" x 29"
$15.00 (plus $5 shipping)

Bartending for Dummies
$15.99 (plus $3 shipping)

The one and only
"BEARTENDER"
(11" tall) $20.00
(includes shipping)

Credit card orders phone: 1-800-46-DRINK (9:00am – 9:00pm M-F, EST only) Or send, check or money order to: BARTENDER, PO Box 158, Liberty Corner, NJ 07938-9986

CY-BARTENDER

www.bartender.com

Now the authority on-premise and on-line

*Meet and exchange drinks, stories, jokes, jobs,
and contact bartenders from all over the world*

Baroscopes with Madame Vena

Happy Hour — Chat with Other Bartenders

The Best of Bar Jokes

New Drink Ideas

Interesting New Products

Hit the Bullet Hole and Get a Shot

*2003 BARTENDER Cocktail Calendar
What's Your Birthday Drink?*

The Art of LeRoy Neiman

*Links to Companies In Our Industry
Your One Stop for the Best Liquor Sites
Plus Other Establishments*

*BARTENDER Bulletin Board, Add, Send and Receive Messages
from Others with the No. 1 Message Board*

*BARTENDER Magazine Products
Great Presents! Gifts For You and Your Friends*

Contests, Win Money and Free Books

www.bartender.com

The 10 Best Reasons for Being A Bartender T-Shirt

Large or XLarge: $20.00
XXLarge: $25.00
(Shipping Included)

THE 10 BEST REASONS FOR
BEING A BARTENDER

1. You get to stay out late.
2. You give "Last Call" and still drink.
3. No kids allowed.
4. You never go home alone.
5. You know where the restrooms are.
6. Only one Happy Hour a day.
7. You know Hymie Lipshitz personally.
8. You get to reject the songs on the jukebox.
9. You don't have to ask - "Do you want fries with that?"
10. Tips.

Back

Front

Credit card orders phone: 1-800-46-DRINK (9:00am - 9:00pm M-F, EST only)
Or send check or money order to: BARTENDER Magazine
PO Box 158, Liberty Corner, NJ 07938-9986

Shakers with Style

FIRE EXTINGUISHER
Brass nickel-plated outside, silver inside. Original dates back to c. 1930, manufacturer F.C. & Co. Britain. Size: 9 ½" x 4"
$100.00

(includes shipping & handling)

LIGHTHOUSE
Chrome-plated reproduction of a fancy shaker dating back to the mid-1920s. Original made by the U.S. International Silver Company. Very rare, very exclusive, very expensive — even in those days. Solid brass, chrome-plated outside, silver-plated inside, handmade. Size: 14" x 5" $200.00

(includes shipping & handling)

THIRST EXTINGUISHER
Brass nickel-plated outside, silver inside. One of the very costliest of cocktail shakers when introduced into their range by the makers, Asprey's of London. Bottom turns to indicate the drink being mixed. Size: 15" x 4"
$150.00

(includes shipping & handling)

JOY BELL
Bell shaped shaker originally made by the Birmingham silversmiths Hukin & Heath, for Asprey. c. 1935. Brass nickel-plated outside, silver inside. Size: 11" x 6"
$100.00

(includes shipping & handling)

DUMBBELL
With a whiff of Art deco design, Asprey designers must have had fun coming up with this highly efficient and attractive shaker. Brass nickel-plated outside, silver inside. Size: 10 ¼" x 5"
$150.00

(includes shipping & handling)

SHIP LANTERN, STARBOARD (green glass)
Originally by Asprey London, c. 1935. Brass nickel-plated outside, silver inside. Originals are extremely rare. Size: 11" x 6"
$150.00

(includes shipping & handling)

SHIP LANTERN, PORT (red glass)
Originally by Asprey London, c. 1935. Brass nickel-plated outside, silver inside. Originals are extremely rare. Size: 11" x 6"
$150.00

(includes shipping & handling)

TO ORDER: Call 1-800-46 DRINK (1-800-463-7465) to place your credit card order, or send check or money order payable to
Foley Publishing, P.O. Box 158, Liberty Corner, NJ 07938.

Place Your Fabulous Recipes Here:

Place Your Fabulous Recipes Here:

Place Your Fabulous Recipes Here:

Place Your Fabulous Recipes Here:

Place Your Fabulous Recipes Here:

Place Your Fabulous Recipes Here:

Place Your Fabulous Recipes Here:

_____

_____

_____

_____

_____

_____

_____

_____

_____

_____

_____

_____

_____

Place Your Fabulous Recipes Here: